Nurturing Potential in the Kindergarten Years

Nurturing Potential in the Kindergarten Years

A Guide for Teachers, Carers and Parents

Cornelis Boogerd

Floris Books

Translated by Matthew Dexter

First published in 2009 in Dutch by Nearchus CV under the title
Het etherlichaam als pedagogisch instrument in de opvoeding van het kleine kind
Translated from the second edition
First published in English in 2011 by Floris Books

© 2009 Cornelis Boogerd

All rights reserved. No part of this publication may be reproduced in any way without prior permission of Floris Books, 15 Harrison Gardens, Edinburgh
www.florisbooks.co.uk

British Library CIP Data available

ISBN 978-086315-836-0

Printed in Great Britain
by CPI Group (UK) Ltd, Croydon

Contents

Preface by Monique Wortelboer … 9
Introduction … 11

Part I – The Ether World and the Young Child … 13
  1. The Pedagogical Law … 15
  2. From Object Image to Process Image … 21
  3. The Ether Body as a Time Body … 27
  4. The Kindergarten Teacher in the Stream of Time … 35
  5. The Streams of Day and Night … 39

An Angel experience … 44

  6. Goldfinches – Help from the Night … 47
  7. Imitation – How do Young Children Learn? … 52
  8. The Seven Learning Processes in Young Children … 56

Part II – The Four Types of Ether … 67
  9. The Four Types of Ether and the Four Elements … 69
  10. The Four Ethers in Free Play … 77

The Land of Living Gardens … 87

Part III – Habits in the Education of Young Children … 95
  11. The Six Qualities … 97
  12. Habits … 102
  13. Habits and Our Connection to the World … 107
  14. Habits as a Medium for Education … 114
  15. A Practical Example of Individual Research … 121
  16. Designing, Conveying, Maintaining … 127

Part IV – The Group as Etheric Organism — 133
17. The Size of the Group — 135
18. Inner and Outer Space of the Group Organism — 142
19. The Development of the Child Within the Group Organism — 150
20. The Group Organism Through Time — 161
21. The Meaning of the Group for the Young Child — 168
22. Running a Group Together — 174
23. Forming Judgments when Working Together — 181
24. Life forces and Job-sharing — 188

Part V – Reflections — 195
25. Waldorf School Children are Healthier — 197
26. The Pivotal Point — 200
27. Ether Body, Soul and 'I' — 206
28. Afterword — 213

Appendix: some experiences from our workshops — 214
Bibliography — 217

Motto

Omnia sponte fluant, ne sit violentia rebus

(Let everything flow freely, without forcing anything)

J.A. Comenius

Omnia sponte fluant

Text: J.A. Comenius – Music: C.L. Boogerd

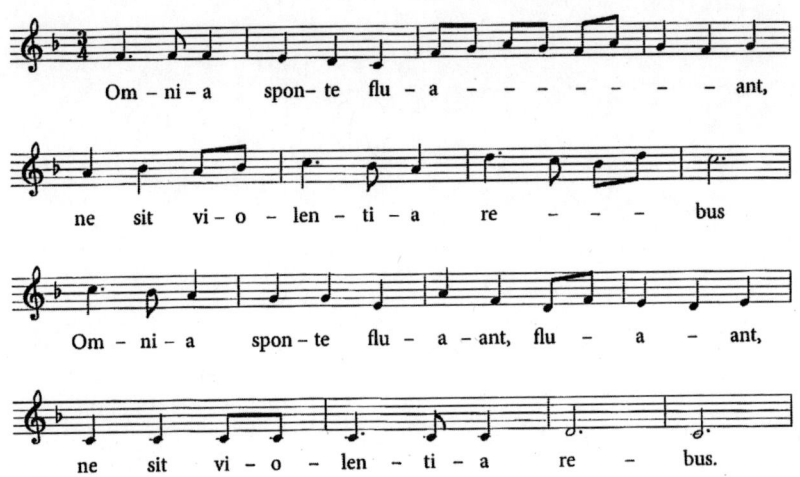

Note:
In all the examples, the names of the children have been changed

In this translation, to avoid the cumbersome "he or she" when referring to a teacher, we have simply used "she" as most kindergarten teachers are female. This is in no way meant to exclude the minority (like the author) who are male.

Preface

This book is the result of pioneering work in developing insights of Rudolf Steiner's Waldorf education. Cornelis Boogerd has given many seminars and workshops for parents and carers of young children and kindergarten teachers in Holland, the Czech Republic and Slovakia. The appendix provides a more detailed description of this work. Some chapters appeared previously as articles in magazines in Holland, Germany and the Czech Republic.

This book aims to help the reader gain a deeper understanding of certain aspects of the ether body, bringing to consciousness something that lives and works in the unconscious. It offers concepts and a method to make the ether world a reality in which we all live: accessible and manageable. The method aims to help children build up their life forces, life forces that are increasingly hindered in their unfolding by certain aspects of modern culture. At the end of each chapter there are questions to encourage your own observations. They can help those working with young children, parents, day-care workers, parent and toddler groups and kindergartens to begin working with the etheric. We are greatly indebted to Cornelis Boogerd for documenting his painstaking labours and offering us the results of his striving to bring this invisible world to light. Readers are shown where to direct their attention to begin observing the ether world, which turns out to be almost disappointingly simple.

The insights offered here can also be applied to help adults work with their life forces and to find harmonious vitality.

I hope this book will help readers deepen their insights into the ether world and that it will help them to work towards a better future for our children and for ourselves.

Monique Wortelboer
March 2009

Introduction

Between concepts and practical reality

Most people find it difficult to form a concrete image of 'the ether body'. And yet it is an important concept in the world-view that is at the heart of Waldorf education. Working with young children in particular, the ether body plays an important role. This book wants to help you to become more familiar with certain aspects of the ether body.

This book does not simply explain certain concepts and relate experiences; it hopes to inspire you to make your own observations, to do your own research. The teachers, carers and parents of young children who took part in our workshops and courses played an important role in developing these insights. I am deeply grateful to them. My gratitude also to Monique Wortelboer who accompanied the development of this book with warm interest.

Anyone who has the privilege to visit a Waldorf kindergarten or parent and toddler group will experience it as a little world of its own. An invisible, living stream flows through, in which the children seem to know their way. They are at home in the many customs and habits and intimately attuned to what goes on, all of which may seem a little enigmatic. The teacher moves within this living stream as a weaving, creating heart. She is connected to all children by invisible threads and her consciousness holds and guides the whole of the group and the stream of activities. This stream, this weaving, the invisible threads, the little customs and traditions, the intimate attuning, are qualities which unfold within the etheric organism of the group of children. So it is vitally important for the teacher to learn to work with the pedagogical effects of the ether world. These effects are not perceptible with our everyday senses. How does the teacher handle them?

On the one hand it is an intuitive, half-conscious, active presence with which she reacts to the ever-changing situation in her class. On the other hand she has learned certain concepts about the ether world in her teacher training. In practical, everyday reality it can be hard to find a connection between this world of concepts and the daily interaction with children. The ether body of the teacher herself makes the connection, but its activity is not perceptible with normal day-consciousness. So how can we learn to deal with it in a conscious way? This book would like to help us make a start.

Kindergartens of today

After a while, anyone visiting a kindergarten may notice that not all children flow easily and naturally within this stream. They come into the group with experiences from a world that often has no room for, or understanding of, this intimate and organic quality. Many modern children have a difficult start in life. The children's world is threatened by haste, violence, uncertainty, divorce, or working parents who have no time for them. Overwhelming and powerful experiences can disturb the equilibrium of children. They are not yet strong enough to deal with these impressions and cannot absorb them properly. They are occupied with other things. To be able to protect themselves from these damaging impressions, they first have to establish a self-supporting, individual organism. Children need the warm surroundings of a family to manage this, surroundings which the kindergarten tries to emulate. It helps children build up a healthy constitution. This group organism has its own dynamics, which can work in a harmonising and constructive way, activating creative forces, and helping to digest experiences. We can imagine and admire the courage it must take to come to the earth as a vulnerable child, carrying an intimate connection with the invisible world into a culture of adults who have, on the whole, lost this connection. In this way, children inspire adults to make room for the source of life and health, which is the ether world. Having an insight into this source is of vital importance for the future of our whole culture.

Are we really willing to truly listen to our children? How can we understand their world? How can we enter anew into the world of creative forces, the ether world, with which the child is so strongly connected? The quest for the true being of the child is, at the same time, a quest for our own being.

Part I

The Ether World and the Young Child

1. The Pedagogical Law

The significance of the ether body for the education of young children derives from the Pedagogical Law, formulated by Rudolf Steiner. To understand this law we have to describe some basic principles of the anthroposophical image of human beings. First of all, there is the insight that the human being does not have just a physical body, but consists of four parts, which do not become manifest at once but are born one after the other, in rhythms of seven years. The ether body is therefore a differentiated area, which will be the focus of this book.

The four births of the human being

The basis for our work in a Waldorf kindergarten is the anthroposophical image of human beings. This recognises four parts of the human being.

1. The physical body, the part that is left when a human being dies.
2. The organism of life forces, ether or etheric body, which maintains the life processes.
3. The soul (or astral body) which establishes consciousness and an inner relationship with the surrounding world.
4. The 'I' of the human being, which directs the three other parts. The 'I' can learn to find its orientation with the help of its spiritual centre, the source of moral orientation.

These four parts come into appearance one after the other in a rhythm of seven-year periods (see also Lievegoed's *Phases of Childhood*).

From birth to the age of seven

During the first seven years a child works mainly on building up its own *physical body*. The body it received from its parents now has to be made more into its own. At birth, its organs have not yet reached their final form: it is the etheric forces which do this. But during this phase the etheric forces are not yet independent: they are highly dependent on the enveloping etheric forces of the child's environment. These provide the child with guidance and orientation for its own formative forces, right down to the formation of its organs. That is the reason children in this phase learn mainly through imitation. Although the child has been born physically, it lives at first in the 'etheric womb' of its environment. If this womb is broken open too soon, for example by a shocking experience, neglect, overwhelming impressions, or a premature appeal to a sense of responsibility, then the vital task of the etheric body to create the individual physical basis for this life is disturbed.

As children lose their milk teeth and gain their adult teeth, this process comes to a conclusion. Of course, all kinds of etheric processes continue: physical growth is not complete. But a base has been formed which makes it possible for part of the etheric forces to become available for consciousness, in the form of an individual memory, for example. Memory is a function of the etheric body, impressions sink into it. Up until the seventh year, memory is not fully and freely available for consciousness, but is bound to outer impressions. Around their seventh year, children reach 'Class 1 readiness' and can start school.

From seven to fourteen

The moment of school readiness announces a second birth: the birth of the ether body, which is now reaching independence. This becomes apparent in new faculties and orientations in the world. A part of the etheric forces is no longer needed for building up the physical body, and becomes available for learning. In *The Education of the Child*, Rudolf Steiner describes six qualities of the ether body, which achieve a more stable and individual form after the seventh year and can become the basis for consciousness: memory, the temperaments, the inclinations, character, habits and conscience. These are all areas which we shall explore in some depth.

Teachers can now begin to educate the part of the ether body that is freed up. One aspect of this is a greater potential for memory, to which we can now appeal for learning. For example, schoolchildren quickly learn the tables of multiplication through rhythmic repetition and games. They open themselves to the world and experience joy in rhythmic games. Habits are another aspect of the ether body. Instilling habits forms the basis for children to be at home within their particular culture. In Part III we shall look closer at these habits.

For children, their schoolteacher is the doorway to the world and they actually enjoy being guided by her authority. In this phase, the soul of the adult guides the unfolding ether body of the child. The soul of the child itself is not yet independent: the soul of the educator acts as an enveloping womb for the soul of the child, which will only be born as an independent entity in the next phase. The teacher must take into account the particular phase of the child's development and uses specific, imaginative, artistic and rhythmical forms of education. In Waldorf schools the letters of the alphabet, for example, are introduced with the help of images, writing with the help of artistic form drawing. Age-appropriate stories also provide children with inner nourishment. Maths classes are enriched by exercises and movement, which help children to experience and understand the qualities and beauty of the world of numbers.

We can discern separate phases within this second seven-year phase. An important moment comes in the ninth year when the child experiences a further inner independence in relation to the world. The world loses part of its lustre; children may, for example, lose their belief in Father Christmas, and begin to notice shortcomings in their teacher.

From fourteen to maturity

In this phase again a new quality breaks through: young people awaken to the world of facts. They begin to form their own judgments, although these may at first be over-simplified. They begin to develop an interest in the opposite sex. After the birth of their own soul qualities, they need security and direction. Peer groups are an important support in this process. They look to adults for ideals, in the search for their own inner ideals. The 'I' of the adult now acts as a womb for the 'I' of the young person, which has not yet been born within the soul. Inner autonomy, truthfulness and enthusiasm are important in this phase. Young people also look for these ideals in adults other than the teacher, and often this is expressed in admiration for music or sports stars. Teenagers in this phase can be quite vocal, but have not yet gained full autonomy and still need guidance.

Around twenty years of age

At this stage, the young person reaches full adulthood and the pedagogical relationship comes to an end. Young people must take responsibility for their own behaviour and development. They may need further guidance, of course, but any advice must respect their freedom.

In many countries a person is considered to be 'of age' at eighteen, when the third seven-year phase has not quite finished. On the one hand this is understandable, as young people take part in society at an ever earlier age. On the other hand, more and more youngsters find the transition to adulthood difficult. This may be related to the fact that superficially the transition takes place earlier, while their inner development cannot keep up. The development of free will, in particular, is under pressure in our consumer culture. Technological devices have taken over many forms of human activity. All this requires extra effort in education, to encourage an adequate development of will power.

Adult life

The seven-year development phases are continuous and interrelated, and continue into adult life. What was developed in the first seven years, for example, forms the basis for possibilities in the phase from age 35 to 42; which in turn affects us from age 56 to 63. Other books have dealt with those phases; we shall confine ourselves here to phases in the development of young children.

The Pedagogical Law

Rudolf Steiner formulated the Pedagogical Law based on the development of the four essential bodies of the human being. In each of the seven-year phases, one particular part of the human being is developed. Each stage requires adult support from the next stage 'up'. So for example, as we have seen, in the first seven years children are mainly building up their physical body. The stage above the physical body is the *ether body*, so the ether body of the adult is the educator of the child. In other words: the ether body is the pedagogical tool. For schoolchildren from seven to thirteen years, who have already built up their ether body, the *soul* of the educator is the pedagogical tool. And for the education of young people of fourteen upwards, the 'I' of the adult is the tool.

For adult self-education, the same Pedagogical Law applies. For example, if we want to work on our ether body, we have to work from the part immediately above that, which is the soul (astral body).

The ether body of the kindergarten teacher

For teachers and educators of young children, the ether body is the main pedagogical tool. This may sound beautiful, and important, but what exactly does it mean? It can be hard to relate the theories we have read about to the daily reality of children in a classroom. The concepts, even if we remember them all, often remain schematic. How can we find a bridge between these concepts and the actual work with children? On the whole our ether body works unconsciously. How can we nevertheless find a conscious relationship to it?

Do we know what our ether body actually looks like? If it is the main medium for education we ought to have some sort of concrete image of it. And how can this elusive ether body be formed into a tool for education? These questions are not meant to be discouraging. In everyday life many parents and teachers already work with their ether body. When we work with a lot of warmth and joy on small things, when we work with regularity, repetition and caring attention, we create a good 'etheric nest' in which children can flourish. These 'motherly' qualities, however, are under increasing pressure today. Both children and educators are threatened by a culture that has lost its connection with the etheric world and which results in many more children needing extra attention, because they have been drawn out of their natural sphere. For parents and teachers too this 'motherly' element is not always naturally present. Increasingly we have to observe and care for it consciously. Kindergartens, day care and other childcare facilities are a modern phenomenon, and in many ways are a mother-replacement. This make it even more urgent for a teacher to work on herself, and in particular to get to know the parts of the human constitution used when working with children.

As an aside, the term 'pedagogical tool' is not ideal. 'Tool' suggests something that allows our will to shape material. What we have described as 'motherly' qualities are more caring and enveloping than the word 'tool' implies. Besides, an etheric relationship with children is not one-way: it is more like an atmosphere between carer and child, where both are active and both grow. In that sense we could also refer to the ether body as 'pedagogical medium'. However, the increasing necessity of using the ether body more consciously and in a more focused way, justifies in my view the phrase 'pedagogical tool,' especially in professional situations. But it is always good to keep these observations in mind.

Awareness among teachers

The patterns of the Pedagogical Law are extremely important, but on the whole teachers are insufficiently aware of them. We should naturally recognise the difference between kindergarten teachers and other teachers, who work with different parts of their constitution. These differences can even be amusing, but they can also cause tensions. How can we work with these differences creatively in a mixed group of teachers? Can we acknowledge the (pedagogical) importance of the different qualities? Is it useful to take these qualities into account outside the classroom situation? And what does it mean for the way teachers work together? We must consciously address questions like these.

2. From Object Image to Process Image

How can the ether body be developed into a pedagogical tool? The ether body is a complex realm with many facets, which can all be researched in more depth. In this chapter we shall first look at some general qualities of the ether body.

The age we live in is deeply materialistic, more perhaps than we realise. Everyone living in the present age is confronted with this. It takes time to recognise it in ourselves, and to develop a different view of the world. The ether world is a realm directly 'above' physical reality (although that is not quite the right description). Above and below are concepts derived from the physical world of space, as is spatial separation. In the etheric world, which interpenetrates physical reality, these principles are not valid. This is an important insight to begin with – but what does it mean in a practical sense?

A little cloud

Mothers will know the feeling when they are separated in space from their young children, for example when they have to work, or go on a visit and leave their child with someone. In some way the child is still present. A mother remains concerned with the child and often senses at a distance how the child is doing, and vice versa. Mother and child are strongly connected within a common 'ether cloud', which slowly dissolves as the ether body of the child becomes more independent and more bound to its own physical body. This feeling of being surrounded by a little etheric cloud can also arise in a group of toddlers. How do we perceive that? To answer that question we have to describe the little cloud in a bit more detail, and see what is at work in the ether body.

One aspect of the ether body is our habits. What are the habits of the little ether cloud? A group of young children, and a family too, can develop their own organism of habits. It is amazing how young children can switch from one ether cloud to another, for example when they leave home for the kindergarten, or when they visit grandparents who have a different set of habits. Through these habits children absorb different cultural references into their etheric bodies, mainly by imitation. It is possible to lay down these habits consciously; in fact, it's often necessary to create certain habits in a class or a family. Without them, life can easily get in a muddle. We only touch upon habits here as part of this overview, in Part III we shall take a closer look.

It is clear that we cannot perceive the ether body with physical eyes, but that we *can* discuss it in a meaningful way. It is possible to bring clarity to real supersensory experiences and to discuss them.

The stream

In their training, teachers learn about all the activities that are part of a Waldorf kindergarten. A teacher has to know a repertoire of songs, movement games and fairy tales. She has to be able to paint and do crafts with the children; has to know the background to all the festivals of the year and practical ways to celebrate them – quite a lot. But if she leaves it at that, a certain rigidity may become apparent after a while. She can learn more, different fairy tales, which is fine, but does it keep her inwardly mobile? It is easy to fall prey to materialistic concepts, although it may not be obvious. We can, for instance, begin to look at separate activities almost as 'objects', one next to the other. The image we have of our day will then be a programme, consisting of separate activities, and they can become a goal in themselves; after all, we have to fill the day somehow. This used to happen in an extreme way in Eastern European communist countries: a central authority prescribed a programme for all kindergartens, which had to be strictly adhered to. Obviously such a system feels very oppressive. But are we ourselves really free from such a way of working?

Families too have a daily programme, with all kinds of activities. In recent years this programme has often become busier and busier. Both parents may now have jobs away from home. Many children have a programme designed to fill the 'empty spaces' in the day: they go to clubs, music lessons, ballet classes, and sport clubs or after school care. The picture of a day as a schedule of activities is becoming more and more prominent. Of course there must be some sort of programme; but if it becomes too fixed, something is lost. What we miss are the times in between, not filled with anything – the transitions and moments of rest, a feeling for the difference between morning, afternoon and evening. We miss a feeling for time as an organic process, with a flow of its own, with rhythms of rest and activity. Related to that is a feeling for allowing time for certain things, letting things run their own course, and really finishing before beginning something new. We shall come back to this later.

It is possible to see a day as something other than a schedule of activities. I like the image of a *stream*. It can be useful to see the course of a day as a stream flowing through all the activities. Like our little etheric cloud, this stream is a supersensory phenomenon, but we do have a feeling for it. It can be very instructive to look back on our day, and to ask how this stream manifested itself. When was it faster, when slower? When was it strong and when weak? When did it threaten to burst its banks and when did it come to rest? What rhythms were there in the stream? We'll come back to the stream in more detail later.

The ether body as a body of time

The stream itself is invisible. It unfolds in time. That is another important quality of the ether body; it is a *body of time*. All etheric processes take place in time. As a teacher or carer we can ask how we ourselves are connected to this stream. The answer will tell us something about our own ether body. Do things often go too fast for our liking, or too slow? Do we tend to break our banks, or do we tend towards stillness? How do we deal with that? Are we able to round things off quietly, letting the echoes die away peacefully? How do we deal with the transition between activities? Do we inwardly sense the process as a whole, for example when telling a story, or do we lose ourselves in the moment? If you're a teacher, do you have a sense for attuning different activities in relation to time, for example when it is nearly time for parents to pick up their children? Handling activities in time means that we move within the stream of the ether.

The ether body as educator

Keeping in mind the main Pedagogical Law which tells us that the ether body is the pedagogical tool for bringing up young children, the question arises: how do we treat our own ether body when working with children? What does it mean that the children have to swim in our 'etheric pond' and have to adapt to us? Does that mean they have to follow our etheric mood, or is there another way? Can we use our ether body in such a way that it serves the children's needs at a particular moment – and how?

Many of these questions already exist in a half-conscious way, and that brings us to a very specific dilemma for people working with young children. On the one hand they are asked to form an etheric unity with the children, and in the etheric our consciousness is asleep. At the same time the teacher or parent cannot allow herself be carried along (like the children). She has to guide the stream, to a certain extent, which demands a wakeful consciousness. Teachers must learn to unite those two aspects more and more. The ether world will then become an 'in-between world' uniting teacher and child, where both take part in their own way. A lot more research is needed in this field and this is something we are trying to begin in our workshops.

Object image or process image

Let us look again at the course of the day. A programme of activities is one way of looking at the day, the image of a stream is another. How does the stream itself want to be? What stream-qualities do we begin the day with, what qualities do we end with? If we can form an increasingly strong image of the stream of the day, the activities within it will acquire a different value. They will no longer be isolated events, but can be judged in relation to the stream.

> *In one workshop in Holland everyone agreed on the purpose of the first activity of the day: it must bring the children together and lead them into the group as a whole. Teachers working with a 'programme image' of the day usually chose an activity where the children sat in a circle and told about their experiences, perhaps to the class gnome. One teacher felt her group was never peaceful enough for this, that the children were still too active; the step to the resting circle-form was too big for several of them. Another teacher described how she always began the day with a short free playtime (with certain definite boundaries), accommodating the different streams the children were still in, and bringing them into a circle out of movement. This approach worked very well.*

So working with the process or stream image of the day, we may shape the day differently from when we use an object or programme image, which has a more solid quality. From the perspective of a fixed-programme image, free play is an activity that allows space for individual creative forces, and usually takes place later in the day. From the process image, a short moment of free play can here serve the needs of the process.

There are no hard and fast rules. It can be interesting to observe our own children or group and discover solutions for a particular situation. In this respect it is important to develop a feeling for the stream, a way of perceiving the processes within the stream. That will allow us to react to every situation in a free and effective way.

These two approaches are like the different ways of observing plants: in a materialistic or an organic way. Modern science observes the separate physical details of a plant, leading to an object image of it. But science has no idea what unifies the parts into a whole. That is what the ether forces do. They bring substances to a 'higher' level and keep them in a state of mobility. In this way, ether forces can work magic on substance. They give it form, unity, life and growth.

We can train ourselves to understand the separate activities of a day in a kindergarten group as a mobile, cohesive unity, and to mould forms and rhythms within this flow. Kindergarten teachers and carers do that with their ether body. It makes the teacher a creative part of the stream; she does not stand outside it. It is a lofty task for the future, for the kindergarten teacher to learn to weave this magic. And she is not alone in this. Etheric beings like the elves, nymphs and gnomes love lending a helping hand. We shall come back to this in Chapter 16.

Questions for your own research

Reflect on a period of time in the day and ask:
How did the stream reveal itself?
Where was the flow rapid, slow, strong or weak?
How was I connected to the stream?
Where did I feel it was too fast, and where too slow?
Do I tend more towards a slow stream, or do I overflow?
To what extent do I influence the tempo and rhythm of the stream?

> How were the children connected to the stream?
> Were they attuned to my own feeling for the stream, or were there differences and tensions?
> How did I handle those?
> In what situations do I go with the general flow of the group, and where do I hold on to my own stream as direction for the whole?
> Can I let go of my own feeling of the stream and change it, if a situation asks for it?
> How do I make such a transition?
> What happens in those situations, what do I need?

3. The Ether Body as a Time Body

In the previous chapter we talked about two ways of looking at the world: as object and as process. By way of illustration we looked at the course of the day. We can either view it as a sequence of separate activities or as a living stream. Looked at as a stream we can consider how the activities and the stream are attuned to each other. When we form an inner picture of the stream, we can sense whether the individual activities support it like an organic riverbed, or whether they block it and cause the stream to overflow.

Kindergarten or Class 1?

We can also look at the kindergarten from these two points of view: as object – a timetable of activities – or as process, the process of the developing child. Viewed as object, the sequence of activities in the timetable does not seem to matter. When we start a car, we can let the engine run as long as we like, it makes no difference for a machine when we switch it on or off. It is different if we look at it from a process or developmental point of view. We can't take a bird from its egg too early, nor can it wait indefinitely before coming out. It reaches a certain stage in its development, and then it has to break out. As we have seen, at kindergarten, children are in a special stage of their development – they are not yet ready for lower school. The teacher makes use of a different part of her constitution from the lower school teacher: the ether body, rather than the soul.

The body of time as mediator

The image of the stream leads us to the etheric reality, which is invisible but which we sense nevertheless. An important aspect of the etheric is *time*. Etheric processes are in constant movement, and work in time. Therefore we can call the ether body and organism of time. As we have seen, the main Pedagogical Law tells us that the etheric body of the adult is the 'educator' for children up to seven. What does this mean if we consider it from the aspect of time?

Every living organism has a time body, which encompasses different processes. These can be big processes, such as the ether body of the human being, which encompasses its entire lifespan. Or the ether body of the Earth, which encompasses the whole of evolution. But shorter processes too have their own time body, for example the course of a day in kindergarten, or even a ring time game or song. Every organic process has its own time. What does the etheric body do with that? How is it connected to time?

The etheric body acts as mediator between two worlds, which would otherwise remain separate: on the one hand the world of soul and spirit, from which the impulses to act originate; and on the other hand the physical world where the results of activity become outwardly visible. Time comes into being between these two worlds, between impulse and result, between when a process is begun and when it becomes manifest in the physical world – for example, a plant that begins to germinate. There is always an impulse for a process about to manifest itself in the physical world. The plant emerges from this process as a spatial and physical form. But what happens in between?

> *A boy walks around in the classroom, looking for something to do. He finds a box of wooden blocks and begins to play. He places one upon the other, building an ever-higher tower, practising his sense of balance. He looks at the tower and is proud of it. Then something changes in the boy: suddenly he takes a swipe at it, and all the blocks tumble down on the floor. This is repeated several times, until he gets bored, sits down in a corner and looks at the other children. After a while he eagerly helps put the blocks neatly back in their box.*

There is a lot going on here. To begin with there is an urge for activity: the boy places the blocks one on top of the other. Then he throws them down on the floor and starts all over. For an adult who is inclined to look at work in terms of results, this seems pointless. Why destroy a beautiful construction and then begin again? Adults often make comments to children from that perspective. For children, however, this game has a different purpose. They live in their vital forces and these forces are active for example in their metabolic system, where substances are broken down and reconstituted. As a result of the destruction of nutritious substances, energy is released, enabling the creation of something new. In their play, 'destruction' serves the same purpose. Children would become unhappy if they were only allowed to look at the physical results of their work. They live in the processes in time, which alternate between rest and movement, construction and destruction, appearing and disappearing. These are living processes with their own 'time'; we could call it a process time or an organic time.

If we force children to play with their blocks for exactly half an hour clock time, without taking process time into account, we disturb the organic time of the child. If the process is interrupted too soon, children remain restless and dissatisfied, and have to release energy in another way. This happens continuously in our modern zap-culture. Children are not allowed enough time to breathe properly.

If, on the other hand, we force children to keep building and adding blocks until the 30 minutes are over, that too causes stress. We lock them into an activity which they cannot inwardly sustain. This also happens when they are led into a guided process of learning at too young an age, and have to assimilate intellectual content. Children are not given the opportunity to breathe out in time, to open up new sources of energy.

This example shows how important organic or process time is in the education of young children. Again and again we have to find balance in the rhythm between breathing in and breathing out, between room for new impulses and ripening time, repetition, internalising and coming to rest. Children have to learn this rhythmic breathing; that is why Rudolf Steiner called education the art of learning to breathe (or: the art of becoming rhythmical). How does a teacher deal with time? Let us take a closer look at several aspects of the time stream.

The stream from the future

Where does the impulse for a new development come from? Where does the urge of the child come from, to play with the building blocks? Where does the impulse of an adult come from to get up in the morning and bake a cake, play the violin or meditate? Where does the urge come from of a cat to chase a bird? The direction of an urge or impulse can differ greatly; it is certainly not visible, and comes from the soul. All kinds of desires, urges, motives and ideals can move the soul and the soul wants to realise, manifest them in the physical world. These desires are aimed at a *future* situation where the goal has been attained. The soul itself does not have the ability to work on physical substance in such a way to attain the goal: it needs the forces of the ether body to achieve that. Without ether forces I cannot move my body, bake a cake or play the violin. The soul gives instructions that guide the ether forces to action in the physical world.

Within the world of the soul the experience of time may vary or even vanish. We can, for example, have the feeling that time passes slowly or quickly, but the clock time does not vary. We're not observing time, but our own feelings. That may be important but it is also one-sided – the true nature of time remains hidden.

The stream from the past

We are able to picture in our minds a plant as a shape in space. We are so used to this, it is hard to remember that this image in space is not complete. To grasp the plant as a living being we have to form an image of its whole development: the germinating seed, forming of roots, growth of stem and leaves, the slowing of growth during the forming of a bud, the opening of the flower and formation of fruit and seeds.

The wilting and withering of the plant, leaving only the seeds, are also part of the image of the whole cycle. Where has the plant gone? Forming such an image in time takes great effort. We tend to stop at the static image in space: the plant as we see it has actually fallen *out* of time. It has solidified into an object when the forces of time free themselves from it. That is the case with the whole world of physical substance – stone, a piece of metal or a table cannot develop anymore. They can only fall apart, erode, disperse. A stone stops time, solidifies the process in a permanent shape becoming an object. In this way the physical world continuously creates a *past*.

The consciousness of time can also be reduced to its mechanical aspects. That happened in recent history as a result of the introduction of clock time. An atomic clock can measure time with incredible accuracy. This clock time however is derived from an object image of the heavens, of sun and earth in particular. Their movements are calculated as if they were a mechanism. Even in this area, we can try to form an alternative process image of the celestial bodies; and then will they come to life.

Ether forces and time

The two qualities of time we have discussed are not difficult to understand: we are quite familiar with the physical world and with matters of the soul. But what about the ether forces: what do they do? They create a living connection between the two. The soul is constantly in movement, it is not easy to concentrate on an impression, a feeling or an image. The soul is in a constant flux. In the physical world, on the other hand, there is only rest and stagnation: the forms are held, fixed. Physical matter has become dense and can only be brought into movement by higher forms of life.

Let's take another look at the image of the stream. The stream itself is in motion, but it does retain a certain form, a mobile cohesion. In a similar way, the etheric body maintains a balance between stillness and movement, form and chaos. It prevents movement from solidifying, but also prevents cohesion from dissipating. This movement and cohesion are both preserved in the ether body (in memory, for example, which retains impressions; or in habits, which are memories of patterns in previous behaviour, without letting the patterns become totally rigid).

In this way the ether body continuously binds together future and past, not in a random way but in a developmental cohesion. Which brings us back to the bird and the egg. Ether forces bring a development to its organic conclusion, but they also work in phases of the development, which lead step by step to its fulfilment. The soul would like to skip those phases – it wants to satisfy its desires immediately. This becomes very obvious in puberty. But the ether body possesses the wisdom of time. It knows that first a root must be formed before a stem can be grown, and so forth. And above all, it holds the different time phases together in cohesion.

The day as a flowform

So, to get to know the ether world, to develop a sense or an organ of perception for it, we have to practise creating flowing images of time. Experienced kindergarten teachers have usually developed this sense to quite a degree, although it may not immediately be recognised as a faculty. They do not have to look at the clock often; they just know where they are in the stream of a day. For a visitor or trainee that may not be so easy. They have to look at the clock regularly, seeking confirmation from this physical representation of time to know where the stream is. Developing a sense for the flow of the day is a slow process, but is one aspect of training the ether body as a pedagogical tool. (Needless to say, it is not forbidden to look at the clock now and then!)

Within the overall picture of the day, there are many smaller organisms of time, and the day flows through them as though through a series of flowforms. Flowforms are water basins placed in a stepped sequence that guide the water into all kinds of movements (such as lemniscates), before flowing down into the next basin. Every activity can be seen as a basin within a flowform. What happens to the stream when it flows through the 'free play basin'? What happens to it when if flows through the 'telling of a fairy tale basin', or through a 'painting session basin'?

All these flowform basins influence each other. When we begin the day too late for example, a certain wave will travel through all the flowforms. The feeling 'too late' will be passed on, and works through all the other activities. It may create a damming up if, later on, there is less time for free play or ring time. The children will sense this. The feeling may continue to niggle, sometimes even into the following day.

When an activity cannot be rounded off properly, something may linger too. Energy is drawn away.

The 'I' in time

We have explored different kinds of time, connected to the different parts of the human constitution. We can refer to physical time, etheric time, and soul time. How is our 'I' connected to time? The 'I' itself is not bound to time or space. But it is active in time and space in order to achieve its goals. We have to discern between our conscious 'day-I,' and the 'I' working on us during sleep in the form of endeavours of will and morality. This 'night-I' or 'higher-I' also works on our destiny from our environment, for example in people we meet and things that happen to us, seemingly from outside but in reality deeply connected with our development. This night-I is much wiser than the day-I, but it remains unconscious, for example as motives in the will. At some point, our day-I may look back and ask why everything happened the way it did. Why did I come to earth in that particular family, in that particular country? Why did my life take that direction? What was the meaning of all my encounters with different people, or of a certain accident? It seemed to come from without, but does it perhaps have something to do with me in an inner way?

The day-I can try to read the images of its life, discover its themes, and come into a more and more conscious conversation with them. When inner and outer world present an ever increasing coherence, we often call it 'happiness' or a feeling of fulfilment. Periods with a clear direction and periods when we search for a new direction may alternate. Our present culture often frustrates this search for new meaning, so an even stronger I-force is called upon to counter it.

Truly fulfilled time is therefore connected to a harmonisation of inner and outer. The more we are consciously aware of this, the more we can speak of I-time, of the presence of the 'I' within time. Success in this can lead to time being transcended. Past, future and present merge into one, imbued with meaning. That is the ideal of complete I-presence in everything we do, the ideal that we should strive for.

We may not be able to attain this yet, but we can strive in this direction. There may be moments when we can experience something of this quality. To work towards this, we can try to become more conscious of how our own 'I' is present in time. Am I master of my time? Does time slip away from me? Do I feel carried along by events? Does my time feel empty or filled with meaning? Do I sleep through important moments, or do I create meaning in moments that seem empty? How do gadgets influence my time? This is a very important and interesting field for introspective research.

In summary, the ether world lives in the connection between past and future, between the world of the soul and the physical world. In each and every moment of time, this link is created anew. Young children up to seven do not yet have these ether forces independently at their disposal. They still have to learn how to find their way into organic time, process time. That is why it's so important for teachers and parents to care for the phenomenon of time. We can help children by surrounding them with enough of the right quality of time, and of flow, to help them orientate themselves, and teach them to swim within the stream with increasing independence. As we have seen, rhythm and repetition are an important help in this work. They strengthen children's etheric forces, because they help them find their way within time. Throughout this book, we shall often encounter rhythm and repetition.

Questions for your own research

Time past

What forms and structures have we developed within the course of the day?

Where do they support the stream, and where do they hold it back?

Time future

What wishes, desires, hopes and ideals work in me and in the children, as motives?

What sympathies and antipathies do I have in my work, for example for certain children or activities, and how do I handle them?

Organic time

What organic processes can I identify in the course of the day?

What phases can I identify within this?

How am I present within the organism of these processes?

Can I carry through the initial impulse of an activity or does it recede quickly?

Can I empathise with the stream?

Can I have a presentiment of the fulfilment of an activity or of the course of the day, and let it 'echo' for a while?

Can I carry the process as a whole within me, and have a feeling for every moment within it?

Where am I tempted to drop out of the process? For example in seeking support from outer structures (the clock, the concept) or in inner unrest (disturbing feelings and thoughts, desires, fatigue).

How can I re-enter the stream?

'I'-time

In which moments was I completely awake and conscious, for example when I was able to actively imbue them with meaning?

In which moments was I asleep, or just carried along, or was something forced upon me?

Which of these three levels do I pay most attention to, and to which am I less connected? Could I change this?

4. The Kindergarten Teacher in the Stream of Time

In the previous chapters we made a distinction between looking at the course of the day as an object image, where all the activities seem stacked on top of each other, and as a stream or process image, where the flowing stream of time is experienced with all its rhythm and inner movement. A day in a kindergarten can be experienced as a flowing organism. The main theme of this book is how the ether body can be developed as a pedagogical tool. At this stage of the book, it is time to consider how a teacher moves within this stream with her ether body. It is, after all, her ether body that shapes the stream, the forms, and the pace of the group. The children move within this stream. From this perspective we can see two distinct types, two opposites: one moves more strongly in the stream, and the other is more connected to solid forms. We can all sense that in ourselves.

Two types

What happens when the stream forces dominate?

> *Every morning a kindergarten teacher welcomed her children with a game, as the beginning of the communal part of their day. She spoke a short verse about water falling down from the clouds to the earth, accompanied by gestures from the sky down to her feet. She wanted the children to imitate this, to 'land' as it were, and calm down as a group. But the opposite happened. The children enjoyed it so much that they slapped their hands down on the floor, getting even more excited. It always descended into chaos. The teacher wondered what to do.*

What was going on in this case? The children imitated not only the form, but also the inner movement which the teacher showed. She was a very mobile person, and the children imitated her inner example as well, which swept away the forms. The solution was not only to change the forms – the text or outer gestures – but to change the attitude, the inner nature, of the teacher. That is where the actual schooling of the ether body as a pedagogical tool begins.

When the stream is stronger than the riverbed of the form, as in this example, the stream can overflow. The form is swept away, cohesion is lost. There may be a lot of life and movement, a lot of fun perhaps, but it ends in chaos, and is not easily led back into the form. When a teacher has this quality of moving too strongly in the flow, it can act on a group like a tidal wave. The children will also imitate each other, and when a group begins to 'roll' it is difficult to maintain direction and cohesion. Teachers must anticipate these tendencies, and inwardly make a counter movement.

What happens when the solid form begins to dominate?

A kindergarten teacher always prepared her day well. She thought through every single activity, giving her the confidence to maintain order in the group. In spite of this, she was not satisfied. She explained that, for instance, in ring games, the children did not engage easily. She had no idea how to improve this. In our workshop we studied the situation with the help of movement exercises. It turned out she was very insecure and tried to find security in the form. But the form cannot replace the stream.

If a teacher is afraid of water, and does not move with the flow, it may dam up; or the energy may drain away as from a stagnant pool. The stream wants to flow and play. A teacher cannot close herself off: the challenge is to open herself to the stream. She succeeded when she took up an idea one of the children suddenly had, bringing a new element into the game. The children were instantly involved in the game, something had opened up. These are little gifts we may receive working with young children.

So concentration on the form can lead to one-sidedness instantly mirrored by the children. This one-sided concentration on the form was extreme in the kindergartens of communist countries in Eastern Europe. A minutely detailed programme was centrally fixed for all kindergartens. If the programme stated that children had to be in the open air for two hours every day, then all teachers had to do that, even if it was freezing or raining hard. No stream can flow in such a situation: it will become a stagnant pool of dead water.

Handling transitions within the stream

The teacher directs the stream with her ether body. The ether bodies of the children are not yet independent; they have to find an orientation with the help of their environment, especially of their carers. The task is to provide a harmonious balance between movement and rest, form and chaos, cohesion and diversity.

The *transitions* from one activity to another are very important in this respect. What takes place during these transitions? When do we sense a damming up, a waterfall, a dividing, and a flowing out into a quiet lake? How can we handle these moments of transition consciously?

The ether forces have their own overall tendencies, but they are guided from a higher world: from the soul and from the 'I'. The kindergarten teacher brings this higher aspect into the group on various levels:

— By preparing the space, materials, activities, and the ideas (past);
— By consciously guiding the stream with the children (present);
— By assimilating unconscious processes, inspiration and endeavours (future).

In our modern society, there are many social and physical disruptions to the natural flows – stagnant pools or floods. When we work more consciously with streaming rhythmical movements, not only do we create an environment in which children can develop healthily and learn to individualise their ether forces, but we also create the basis for a new culture.

Questions for your own research

Transitions
  Which moments of transition can I sense during the course of a day?
  How am I present during these transitions? How do I guide them?
  Do I let the previous activity linger on a little, or are my feelings already directed to the next activity?

Do I create a space in between the activities? Do I fill them up, or are they open spaces?

Do different activities demand different forms of transition? Can I characterise them?

At which point do I sense the transition in the children?

How do the children move along with my movements? Where do things get stuck, why, and what could I change?

Three levels within the stream of time

Past

How am I engaged in the practical preparations of the activities in the group?

How important is that for me? How precise am I in my preparations?

Do I work from clear concepts and images, do I use practical aids?

Present

How am I present within the actual stream?

Future

Where do I find my inspiration? From looking back – from meditations, sudden inspirations, dreams, moods, new impulses?

How do I transform these inspirations into preparation for the following day?

Which of these three levels is dominant in me, and which less dominant? Am I able to change my emphasis, should a situation call for it?

5. The Streams of Day and Night

In the previous chapters we tried to gain a first understanding of the ether world using the metaphor of a stream. Here we shall attempt to deepen that image.

The kindergarten compared to the course of a stream

Young children swim, as it were, in the streams of the ether sphere, and are guided and nourished by their surroundings. Out of these streams they build up their body. What shapes and movements are visible in this?

In the mornings the children come streaming into kindergarten. What do they bring with them? From which other streams do they come? They look for connection with each other and with the teacher, and sooner or later they flow into a whole. The group then streams through various activities that offer form for this stream. It is interesting to see what these activities do to the stream. When does the stream flow faster, when slower? When is there more cohesion, when does it disperse? How does the group flow out again after a day in kindergarten? What do they take away with them? How do we deal with all these streams as a teacher? How are we connected with them ourselves? We can develop a feeling for these streams if we live with these questions for a while, without attempting to answer them too quickly. It is a different way of looking, different from observing visible events. The stream flows through these events. We could compare it to learning to swim again. We will return to these questions later in this chapter.

From stream to cycle

So far we have followed the image of the stream. Is that the whole picture? How does water continue to flow down from the mountains? Where does all this water come from? Where does rain come from? From clouds of course. If we follow the clouds back to their origin, we see them arising mostly above the sea, where water evaporates and rises up to the heavens. Now we begin to see a second stream that moves in the opposite direction from the river. Water evaporates from the sea, it becomes 'invisible'. Clouds are only formed in the right conditions – of temperature, humidity, dust particles – and are then blown by the wind toward the land. They are forced upward by mountains or currents of air into colder strata, where water droplets form and fall down as rain, hail or snow. This second stream allows the first, visible stream to exist. Together they form a whole, a cycle, in which all kinds of phenomena interact, some supporting each other.

There are many of these cycles and together they form the streaming, flowing organism of the earth. Every little brook, each current in the ocean, each cloud formation is part of that whole. Within this streaming organism of the earth, the ether body of the earth can work. Like all streams and circulations in our body, the streams and currents of the earth work on each other. That presents us with a different image from the image of the earth as a place full of isolated objects. Similarly the etheric organism of a group of young children and their teacher does not have such strictly defined boundaries as those of the physical reality. The ether forces interweave as streams that complement and influence one another. How do we observe these? How do we move in and with these streams?

The streams of day and night

Returning to the image of the day as a stream, we can begin to see its counter stream. In relation to the teacher, this stream begins at the moment of saying goodbye, at the end of the kindergarten day, and flows on until the following morning. What happens during that time? Like seawater evaporating and becoming invisible, the streams flowing beyond the classroom are invisible. They flow within the families of the children and into the night. But this world of the night is part of the whole day. A day is not complete if we do not take the night into account. When we recognise the full cycle of day and night as a flowing organism, we can ask where this cycle really begins. At the moment of waking? In the image of river and sea, water flows toward the deepest point, following gravity. The water could remain there. New movement only begins when enough warmth is generated and this warmth carries the water upward in a counter movement: water is liberated from the gravity of earth. This initiates the entire cycle, which then descends again following gravity. So there are two forces of movement: warmth for the invisible movement away from the earth, and gravity for the visible movement toward the earth. Looking at the cycle like that we might identify the beginning as the moment when the water warms up and evaporates. In the cycle of day-and night, however, that is the moment of falling asleep! The day stream has come to rest and has run its course through the sequence of visible activities. We fall asleep and free ourselves from the visible world. What happens to us during that time? Why are we fit and rested every morning? Which sun has warmed us during the night? What endeavours and ideas, emerging from the night, fall like fertile rain upon our day? The day stream can only resume as a fresh source because of what happens during the night.

Tending the day and night streams

Of course these two streams of day and night affect each other.

The *day stream* lays the foundations for the possibilities of the night stream. How did I close the day? Were any issues left unresolved? If so, I may encounter them again next day. They will have to be dealt with to make room for the new day. If I leave them unresolved for longer, the riverbed of the stream may clog up and I will lose energy and enthusiasm.

But I also bring my inner state with me into the night. How was I present during the day? If there was a lot of stress, or tension, it will be harder to let go of the day. And that will make it harder for me to 'evaporate' into the invisible world where we find inspiration for the next day. The stream of day works on into the night. But we can handle that in an active way, for example by closing off our day consciously and finishing practical things as best as we can. The exercise of *looking back over the day* can be a way of releasing ourselves more consciously, and to go into the night more freely. *Looking ahead* to the coming day also allows us to live through the ideas for the coming day during the night, making them riper and more concrete. We can become more aware of that too. We cannot fix or plan the flow of the following day, but we can create the conditions for it. Why do certain activities run smoothly, others not at all? What connection do I have with them? How can I let the night stream take part in that?

On the other hand, the *night stream* also works on during the day. Waking up we receive fresh energy. Not only that, the night gives us focused endeavours which we look for during the day. They want to be realised, even if they are no longer conscious. I may meet someone with whom I have an important conversation. We had arranged that during the night, when we perceived everything more clearly, but had both forgotten. Many of these important 'coincidences' take place – sometimes we call them miracles but mostly we do not recognise them as such. If we try to be conscious of the moment of waking up, the night may give me new ideas, for instance about a child that has been giving trouble.

So day and night affect each other. In day consciousness we have practically forgotten what we experienced during the night. But it is possible to learn to understand the language of night during the day too. That allows us to engage in active conversation with the night.

At night there are spiritual beings working with us, such as angels, whom we cannot see during the day. I can open myself up to them before going to sleep; through meditation or prayer I can tune in to the world of night. I can ask a child's angel for advice on how to understand and guide the child. The answers may come in various guises: as a sudden inspiration, a new idea or a mood, or they may come from the child itself, indicating what it really needs. Learning to listen to these answers is an art. It is important to trust that the answer will come.

We have deepened the image of the stream. Questions naturally arise which we can use to explore life in our kindergarten. Holding these questions inwardly for a while, we may make our own discoveries, which become our spiritual 'property'. We do not easily forget those discoveries. A process may begin where the world of night increasingly moves along. The beings living in that world are keen to help us but they can only do so properly when we ourselves become active. As we have seen, that all begins with warmth: enthusiasm for guiding our little fellow human beings.

The review

The exercise of reviewing a day can be done in different ways. One way is to imagine ourselves standing on a high mountain looking down on the events of the day, as if we were an outsider. Let the images of the day pass by in reverse order, from the present moment back to the moment we woke up. Looking at ourselves as an interested bystander also means we do not make judgments and remain calm. This helps to detach ourselves and we fall asleep more easily. We learn to observe ourselves and our life in a more objective way, and quickly learn to distinguish what is essential and what is not. It is good to do the exercise over a long period of time, although the exercise itself should not take too long. A lot can be achieved in five minutes: after all, it is an exercise in letting go.

Questions for your own research

The stream of day

How was I present during the day?
Was I able to live in the moment? Could I let go?
Could I vary my degree of concentration according to the demands of the situation? Was my attention diverted, or split? Was I concentrated or easily diverted?
Was I able to create moments of peace?
How did I close the day?
Was I able to round off practical activities?
What did I do with unresolved activities?
Do they occupy my mind before falling asleep? Did I make practical preparations for the next day?
How can I let go before falling asleep? Do I manage an active review? (see below)

The stream of night

Have I made an inner picture of the next day, with several main points?
Do I have certain inner ways of rounding off the day? Meditation, prayer, review, living into an image, picturing the children in my mind's eye?
How do I wake up? Can I experience a moment of rest before the day begins? Can I allow the experiences of the night to work on for a moment? Which experiences that I had during sleep can I experience: dreams, inspirations, impulses, moods?
Are there things I see differently this next day? Are there things I experience as inwardly more full, riper, compared with the previous day?
Can I recognise influences stemming from the night in my day life? How do I create room for that? (For example, creating a space in which people can speak out, or in which unexpected things may happen.)

An Angel Experience

In February 2000 a six year old girl, Adelka, joined our kindergarten. As director of our kindergarten I decided to take her on recommendation of another Waldorf school in the Czech Republic. Adelka was born in the USA to a Czech mother and an Italian father. There were complications during her birth. The caesarean was probably carried out too late, which meant the language areas of her brain were damaged. After birth she experienced the acrimonious divorce of her parents, and several moves between the Czech Republic, Italy and the USA.

Her behaviour in our group astonished us. Every time I wanted to sit down, I had to check that Adelka had not pulled my chair away. We could not let her out of our sight for a single moment. She had no relationship with the other children, or to animals, nature or even objects. If there was any relation at all, it was a negative one. Her characteristic stance was: one leg forward, hands on her hips, chin jutting out, ready for battle.

I had taken on Adelka out of the conviction that Waldorf pedagogy can be very healing. My colleague and I had prepared thoroughly for her joining our group. When she was in the classroom with us, one of us was with the rest of the children while the other concentrated on Adelka. Adelka was extremely creative. We locked the classroom, so that we did not to have to go looking for her all the time, but she turned the tables on us: we were locked in and Adelka ran round the whole school building. Time and again she managed to escape, and each time she would break something or throw things around. Once she took a handful of pins from the notice board, ran to the kitchen and threw them into the soup our cook was making. We had to throw away a pan of soup for seventy children.

She would attack other children with sharp objects, and when we reacted to that, she would take up her characteristic pose, stare at us defiantly and throw toys around. Once I held her firmly round her waist; she looked at me furiously, defended herself and told me that it hurt. I could go on about how she bit us, stole a considerable amount of money, and took favourite toys away from other children. After exactly a month we had had enough. She threw a glass on the floor shattering it into a thousand pieces that flew all over the classroom. A little boy cut himself on one of them. Outside she dragged a little girl around by her necklace. After lunch she smashed her plate in the sink. We could not bear it any longer. I asked her mother to keep her at home for the time being. I wondered who could give us advice about bringing up a girl like this, how we could find a path to her.

During one of the sessions of our workshop Cornelis Boogerd and I reviewed the various possibilities of helping Adelka on different levels: physical, emotional, her personality, social relations and so forth. At the end of our conversation Cornelis suggested I could try establishing a connection with Adelka's angel through my own angel. I did not know that was possible. How can you create such a connection? Cornelis advised me to create a mental image expressing Adelka's being and my question. I did not manage very well. I went into sleep with the image of Adelka as a baby. I fell asleep slowly. At the threshold of waking and sleeping I entered into a kind of hallowed state. I cannot describe it exactly. I felt such an overpowering love descend over me that I could even feel it physically. This was in the region of my head; it seemed to be in a different realm, and my heart, too, reached into this space. Is this what nirvana is like?

I saw myself lying at the edge of a deep well with transparent water. In the middle there were three shapes like tender water lilies. And in the middle of these was the face of Adelka, like a beautiful little girl. I felt this was her true being. Around her were swirling shapes like shredded rags in black, blue-black and dark-grey. I reached in and pulled out these rags, one by one. But they flew back in, swirling round wildly as before.

The next evening when falling asleep, I entered the same hallowed state. Again I was lying beside the well, and saw the flowers in the middle. Now the cloths were moving in a peaceful and harmonious way around her and they had softer colours. After two weeks I took Adelka back into our group. She seemed a totally different girl. She was very quiet and seemed to have her wild temperament under control. She did run quite a lot, but only *in the places and times meant for it. She began to play. She sought physical contact – stroking, cuddling. She also began to speak words. The first word I heard her say was motyl (butterfly). After several weeks she ran up a temperature. She sat by the window waiting for her mother to come, tears streaming down her cheeks. When she was better, she came back. She was very keen to celebrate her birthday immediately. And we fulfilled her wish. Although her birthday wasn't until in December, we celebrated her 'new birth'. She stayed with us for the rest of the year. Everyone loved her – the teachers, children, co-workers and parents. She behaved just like the other children. She played with them, joined in the ring time games and listened to the fairy tales. But she hardly spoke. Now and then she would say a word, but did not follow it up. In spite of that she, the other children and the teachers could understand each other well.*

V.S., Waldorf kindergarten teacher, Czech Republic

6. Goldfinches – Help from the Night

A child comes to earth with certain intentions and potential. Parts of the ether body are ether forces working on from a previous life. They mingle with the ether forces the child was given by its parents. Children want to go through certain experiences here on earth, which they carry with them in unconscious images of will. Part of these images of will have a general human nature, for example the will to become human in a physical constitution. And part have a more individual nature, for example the individual tasks for this life. Children seek an environment where they can have certain important experiences, so they can develop an ether body capable of fulfilling the individual tasks for this life. (The traditional childhood diseases, for example, are experiences a child actually looks for, during which it transforms the constitution received from its parents, tuning it to its own intentions and possibilities.)

The environment where children are born and grow up, the parental home, people, culture, geography, lead to the desired experiences for children's development. In this respect, what the environment of our materialistic culture has to offer is problematic. The growing number of children that cannot take advantage of what is offered to them, either at home or in the classroom, is testimony to this. They demand extra attention from parents and teachers. What can we do for these children?

In the first seven years children mainly builds up their own physical constitution. The forces active in this process are the ether forces. Children surrender themselves to their environment in imitation. If the environment offers images children cannot use for their development, problems will arise which can manifest themselves in many ways.

Children face disturbing, overwhelming and dramatic impressions, images and experiences in our modern age which is increasingly losing its connection to the nourishing ether world. This can cause all kinds of problems, such as allergies, asthma, and hyperactive or autistic tendencies, and a weakening of the immune system.

In Waldorf kindergartens we try to offer an environment attuned to the children and their needs. This is an important cultural task. If a good foundation can be laid in the first seven years, then as an adult we can fall back on this. Without this foundation it will be difficult to function properly as a healthy human being with today's stress and demands. People are easily torn apart. Stress, burnout, depression and other problems of our age are witness to this. Research in England has shown that young children do best when they stay with their mother.* Over a period of seven years 1200 children were studied in different kinds of care. Children who were not cared for by their parents often became more aggressive, less cheerful, more withdrawn and complained more.

However, many children go to day care. It is important that qualities that are good for the child are fostered there.

Waldorf parent and toddler groups and kindergartens provide an environment that stimulates the ether forces, for example in rhythms which breath through the day. We can see how nourishing the magic of the ether stream is for a group of young children. On the other hand there are children who have already had intense experiences, are oversensitive, overburdened or damaged in some way. They too can benefit from the ether forces of the group, and often find a new balance in them. But sometimes a child needs something more, for example when it does not manage to join in with this stream.

Goldfinches

It can be very painful to have a child in our group who somehow does not manage. Whatever we try – stimulating him or leaving him alone – nothing seems to work. We feel powerless. We may, however, receive help in such moments, through an inspiration for example. I call these gifts *goldfinches*. Gold because they are wise and healing, and finches because it feels as if these images are 'sung' to us from another world, like an inspiration. We have to be open to hear them.

There are several qualities a goldfinch must have, before I call it a goldfinch:

— It must be an image expressing the inner state of the child.

---

* Yvonne Roberts, 'Official: babies do better with mother,' *The Observer*, Oct 2, 2005.

— The image must get a physical form, because the physical world gives the child its experiences. Fairy tale imagesare also effective of course. But for many children transforming these images into processes and deeds is actually the problem.
— The image must have a enveloping quality, which leaves the actual process to the child itself. Of course, the kindergarten teacher has to be present and follow with warm attention.
— Often these inspirations appear when there is pressure, an emergency, or when a solution seems far away.

Anyone who has ever experienced a 'goldfinch' will not likely forget it. The child and the teacher can experience great joy in these moments. Here are two examples.

Bananas

Stan was a little blonde boy who had just turned four. He had had a very difficult start in a toddler group somewhere in the west of Holland, and sadly the teacher had asked his parents to take him out of her group. Then he moved near us and with some trepidation he and his mother came to the kindergarten. At first they came for an hour or so at a time, then gradually longer, the whole morning, and soon without his mother.

He was very awake, sensitive and perceptive. You could tell his mood by the colour of his cheeks. He would arrive in the kindergarten quite pale and gradually his cheeks would become red. One morning when he came in he was passive. He sat on his little chair fairly pale and withdrawn and he looked quite worried when I asked him whether he wanted to go to 'play-land'.

I recognised this mood from when he had just joined and was afraid he would relapse into heavy, negative moods, so I had to think of something in the moment.

I was just peeling fruit and asked if he would like to 'help the bananas take their coats off'. He looked a bit worried at first, but then he jumped up from his chair and came over. His expression and the colour of his cheeks changed instantly. His cheeks turned red and he began to 'flow' again.

The following days he continued helping me with the bananas, and now has a good start every day.

H.L., kindergarten teacher, Holland

Walnuts

Several years ago I was visiting a kindergarten in Slovakia, with a Dutch kindergarten teacher. There was a little boy in the group who never joined in with anything. It was impossible to get him moving. He had had all kinds of therapies. His mother was a psychologist herself and was at a loss what to do. The Slovak teachers were also at their wits end. The Dutch kindergarten teacher took this image with her into sleep, wondering what might help the child.

Next morning while showering, she had a brainwave: a walnut! She was immediately convinced this could help. It turned out there actually were some walnuts in the classroom. The boy was allowed to crack the walnuts, and the other children had to watch. The walnuts were meant for a cake that was to be baked that morning. The boy was immediately gripped by this activity. He was totally absorbed, cracking the nuts with a little hammer. It was quite a job, but in the end he managed. Everyone was very pleased, the boy most of all. He went on, cracking one nut after the other, while the other children came and fetched them for the cake. That is how he overcame his inner oppression. The next day his excited mother asked the teachers: 'What have you done with him? He is totally changed, it is a miracle!'

It was a miracle, there is no doubt about that. But the ideas of Waldorf pedagogy did help this miracle along a little. There are many wonders in this world. The beings that make them possible hope that we notice them – they could work many more wonders if we were more open to them. These goldfinches are inspirations from another realm. With our ordinary day consciousness we cannot perceive this other world. At night we return there, but in the morning we have forgotten everything we experienced, who we met, what important impressions we received.

As we described above, an everyday situation can suddenly become a telling *image* of the inner state of a child, and can help us offer an environment where the child can take a step in his or her development.

Peeling a banana, cracking a hard shell, become images of victory over an inner block. Everyday reality becomes much more vibrant when we recognise the imaginative language speaking through it. From the perspective of the night, this imaginative language is more real than the outer events.

It is possible, through meditation, to gain conscious entry into the night world. This meditative concentration does require effort. Sometimes we make this effort in an emergency when we cannot see our way through, concentrating our whole being on a particular question. Regular practice helps strengthen the power that allows us increasingly to enter into dialogue with the night world, and to receive essential images and inspiration which give everyday life deeper meaning.

7. Imitation – How do Young Children Learn?

We all know the setting: a mother at her ironing board and a four-year-old child imitating her at a little plank with a block of wood and some handkerchiefs.

Young children do not yet feel totally separated from their environment. They live deeply within it. Moving along on an inner and on an outer level, they acquire many skills which only later become more conscious. Young children therefore learn through *imitation*. Conscious school learning does not work for them yet, because that is based on the artificial separation between a learning environment and everyday life. This separation is not a reality for a child. That is why Rudolf Steiner said imitation was the magic word for the education of children during their first seven years.

Sounds beautiful, but what does in mean in practice? And isn't there a great difference between children of one year and children of six?

From birth to three years

Imitation is a wonderful faculty. Human beings are born with it; we bring it with us from the world we come from. Initially a baby in its cot is brought into movement by its organism, its metabolism and natural reflexes. That is the first area where it must make itself at home. For animals, to a point, that is the end of their development. They are so strongly defined by their instincts that they soon reach maturity and can behave in the same way their parents do. For a human being this process is much slower. Children need a year to raise themselves into the vertical (to be able to walk). Without an example to follow, they cannot manage this. Just think of all the things children have learned by the age of three! They have to learn to move their body of their own volition, they have to learn to speak the way people in their environment speak, and they have taken the first steps toward forming their own thoughts.

It is often very funny to notice how children acquire all kinds of subtle idiosyncrasies from their parents: their movements, pronunciation and quite often something of their attitude to life. With their whole being children strive toward becoming human in the most general sense of the word. And if the human beings in their environment walk with a slight stoop and, perhaps, a Yorkshire accent, the children will adopt this too, without even studying a textbook!

From three to five

When children have built this foundation, they can become more open toward their environment. They start to form inner pictures of this environment, which allows them to begin empathising and sympathising with them. They are happy when they see familiar images, familiar people, furniture, toys, and a familiar picture book, which they can enjoy time and again. Children begin to draw their first pictures.

Toddlers will at first look on dreamily when older children are playing. Little by little they begin to move and join in. They love this connection with other children, adults and nature. They now come into active conversation with their surroundings. This is the golden time of imitation: we can see it in a group of young children in a circle around their kindergarten teacher. They imitate her gestures with great joy: a sunflower opening, rain falling from the clouds. When the teacher picks a bit of fluff from her sweater, the children will imitate that too, unquestioningly and with equal pleasure. Imitation is immediately visible now.

From five to seven years

Something begins to change as the children grow older. They no longer follow so naturally and have their own concerns: 'I don't have time now, I am a bus driver!' or 'Alright, I will help you lay the table, but can I finish my puzzle then?' They are becoming school children. Their interests become more personal and they become more selective in their imitation. Increasingly they place their own thoughts and considerations between observation and action. They may now replay a visit to the zoo or the dentist later, possibly giving the story a new twist. They can do this, because they are slowly learning to bring their memory under control.

A slightly older child needs examples it can identify with. For this reason it is valuable to let a child in this phase experience various images of professions and meaningful activities. Active examples especially are a great gift.

Lower school

Children are only able to manage more conscious considerations when they are ready for Class 1. They can then begin a different way of learning. In lower school the teacher can appeal to the children's independent memory. They are able to perform a task in another environment and at another time. They can begin to learn consciously in a learning environment different from their everyday reality. The capacity for imitation begins to diminish, although parents and teachers may appeal to it until the age of nine.

The teacher

It is quite important to be aware of these differences in a child. If, for example, we expect a child of six to imitate in the same way as a four-year-old, we will often be disappointed, and we place unnecessary pressure on the child. Sometimes we can appeal to a child of six in a more direct way.

What do these insights mean for a teacher? They are beautiful theories, but reality can be quite confrontational. The example of the teacher with some fluff on her sweater is quite amusing. But what if the children imitate things we'd rather they did not? Our behaviour as a teacher suddenly acquires a different dimension. Things we usually do quite unconsciously suddenly become examples for the little human beings around us. How do we deal with that? We are confronted with our own limitations as a human being, which can be difficult. But children will also perceive when we are honest with ourselves and the world and try to learn from our shortcomings. That too is an example from which they can learn.

It is not only the children who learn: the adult learns too. Living with a child gives us the opportunity to re-examine certain themes in our own development:

— How do *I* relate to nature, to creation, to my own body?
 What example do I set with regard to these?

— How do *I* relate to other people? Can I experience joy in being together with others, in the play of interaction?
— What do *I* identify with? What are my strengths? What do I admire?

We may be confronted with certain issues from our own childhood. The teacher's path gives us a chance to address these. We are not alone on this path. We have the best teachers we could wish for: young children.

8. The Seven Learning Processes in Young Children

The health-bringing effects of a good Waldorf education are related to the deep insights into the nature of the human being underlying it. These are not dogmas, but a living world that is in constant development. And there are many more discoveries to be made. Questions are asked and in the interaction between people, new insights will be developed. In recent years many in the Waldorf movement were interested in the seven learning processes. Rudolf Steiner recognised in these the transformation of the seven life processes working in the human organism, but he only gave brief indications. Years later several people rediscovered this theme and developed it in more detail. The first was probably Christof Lindenau, then later Coenraad van Houten and Edmond Schoorel, and the idea of the seven learning processes became the foundation for what was called 'source pedagogy' in Holland. An understanding of the seven life processes has proved to be very effective in Waldorf pedagogy.

The seven life processes

1. Breathing
2. Warming
3. Nourishing
4. Secreting
5. Maintaining and renewing
6. Growing
7. Reproducing

1. Breathing
Breathing is our first encounter with the outside world. In the membranes of the lungs a very subtle meeting takes place, between the air of the atmosphere and the blood absorbing the oxygen.

The way a child breathes is an indication of the way it absorbs impressions from the outer world. The superfluous and provocative impressions children are exposed to now can cause or aggravate complaints like asthma: they cannot breathe out anymore, leaving no space for a fresh breath. Through a rhythmical dosage of impressions, in waking and sleeping, and in various activities, a child is helped to learn to breathe and to open and close itself again to its environment in a harmonious way.

2. Warming

Warming is a more inward process than breathing and is related to inner warmth and morality. The involvement of the child in what it does and in the activities of the adults around it, allows it to connect to and love its environment. Rudolf Steiner wrote about the warmth of the educator: 'Such a love that streams ... with warmth through the physical environment of the child may be said to literally "hatch" the forms of the physical organs'.* Warming is an important life process and must be well cared for. Warming, like breathing, is interactive, attuning to the warmth of the environment. Warmth is mainly carried and distributed by the blood.

3. Nourishing

Nourishing is the third life process. Here the environment penetrates the organism more deeply. Strength is required to handle all these substances. This strength is aggressive by nature. Food is broken down in several phases, from chewing to the working of gastric acid in the stomach and the movements of the intestines. The organism needs these abilities to maintain itself within the environment. In encountering these external substances children get to know the outer world. From the life forces in good, healthy nourishment, they learn to overcome what is harmful, to transform what is useful, and to build up their own substances. The organism becomes capable of maintaining itself on the earth and building up its own life forces.

4. Secreting

The fourth life process is the ability to discern what belongs to us and what does not. In other words what can be absorbed, assimilated and integrated, and what has to be rejected and excreted. This ability is also active, with great wisdom, in the other life processes.

---

* *The Education of the Child* p. 22

5. Maintaining and renewing

This life process maintains the relations and proportions within the body. These have to be given new life again and again to maintain their form and function. Left to itself, the body would disintegrate. These constructive forces are gained through the breaking down forces of the third life process, nourishing.

6. Growing

Growth means more than just an increase in size. At every phase of growth new proportions have to be brought into harmony with the whole, for example, by ensuring that one leg does not grow faster than the other. Growth is actually a kind of 'social' process in relation to the organism. Here too we can admire the active wisdom with which our body is built up and maintained.

7. Reproducing

Reproduction, the physical capacity to create a new organism, is only latently present in young children. The creative forces are separated into masculine and feminine qualities. Animals pass rapidly from childhood into the adult phase. In human development there is a long period between early childhood and sexual maturity. This holding back gives school children another seven years of freedom, to learn and to form an individuality not totally defined by their species.

The seven life processes are an organic whole with qualitative cohesion in their sequence and their mutual relations. The first three life processes for example are movements from outside to inside, where impressions and substances are absorbed into the organism. In the last three there is a movement from inside to outside: what was received from outside is assimilated and transformed into new creative abilities. The fourth life process is active within all other life processes as the ability to discern what can and what cannot be assimilated into the body.

The seven learning processes

Now let us look at the seven learning processes, which are transformations of the seven life processes. As we have seen, the seven life processes are about the absorption, transformation and integration of substances from the outer world. In a similar way the seven learning processes are about the absorption, transformation and integration of *learning content*. The seven learning processes are:

1. Taking in, perceiving
2. Connecting, recognising
3. Researching, analysing
4. Individualising, judging
5. Practising, renewing
6. Growth, expanding
7. Creating, creative application

1. Taking in, perceiving
The first learning process, the transformation of breathing, is the first impression we receive of something, the *perception* of the content; for example, a new song we hear. Perception is very important for the learning process. Without good perception the other learning processes cannot bear fruit. On the other hand the learning process would be limited if it stopped at outer perception, without forming a meaningful relation to it.

2. Connecting, recognising
The second learning process, the transformation of warming, is the capacity to be interested in the learning content, the new song, and to form a *connection* to it. It is important that after the first perception a relationship is developed to the subject matter. If we stop at outer perception, we won't be able to play the song on the violin. We must become inwardly mobile through a warm interest in the song.

3. Researching, analysing
In learning, the process of feeding becomes the capacity to *analyse* the learning content, to explore it further. To learn the song we have to take it apart carefully. We divide it into several parts, each with their own character and style. What intervals, rhythms and musical qualities do we hear in the new song? We have to keep an eye on the notes to find out when to play legato or staccato.

4. Individualising, judging
The ability to *discern* in the fourth learning process is related to the question of whether the content is absorbed or not. Do I want to

assimilate this content, this song, to make it part of myself? Does it belong to me, or do I put it aside? The fourth learning process is an instrument of the 'I'. Asking questions is an important part of this process. There is an inversion here: what came from outside must first be assimilated inwardly, until the capacity is developed to bring it forth creatively from the inner world back to the outer world. This is when the second half of the learning process begins, where the will is increasingly called upon.

5. Practising, renewing

Once we have made up our mind, the new capacity has to be maintained, to make sure we hold on to it and not lose it. Our own coherent image of the new song must be brought to life and *practised* repeatedly until it comes out effortlessly. The song we have learned is made familiar in this fifth learning process. It is not enough to listen to and analyse it. We have to make it our own in such a way that we no longer have to think about technique and annotations. Repetition makes it a part of our own ether body.

6. Growth, expanding

The sixth learning process incorporates the new ability within the whole of our abilities. This process of *including*, of attuning, is always musical, even if it does not concern a musical ability. In our example the new song finds its place among the other songs, melodies and techniques we had acquired before. These abilities fructify each other and they grow into a whole: my musical capacity.

7. Creating, creative application

Ultimately the learning process leads to a new *ability* that can be used creatively in the world. The song has become so much part or ourselves that we can play it very well and perhaps even create new songs. The path has led from inner world into the outer, a path mainly of the will. The process continues further into the outer world as a creation with its *own identity*.

This example shows that a complete learning process always includes on the one hand absorbing, transforming and integrating of learning content, and on the other hand the development of new abilities.

Inverting the sequence of the learning processes?

So far it all seems straightforward. But there is some lack of clarity about the working of the learning processes in young children up to seven. How do children learn before the age of seven?

If we observe the development of young children we see that they gradually become more conscious, but that they mainly live and learn through doing. What does that mean for the seven learning processes? Do they not apply to the first seven years, or do they somehow appear in different guises? Some authors have come to the conclusion that in young children the seven learning processes appear *in reverse order*. Normally, learning processes lead from observation to the ability to create something new, whereas in the development of young children, *action* comes first. What is usually the seventh and last process, for young children comes as the first: *creative activity*. And that what is usually the last learning process for children comes first: *perceiving*. This seems logical, but is that really how it works?

We saw that learning processes are about the absorption, transformation and integration of learning content, which can then be transformed into a *new ability*. This ability can be a certain action, or it can be an ability to feel or to think. But is perception really an ability – acquired as the end result of every path of learning? This would only make sense if perception wasn't present before. For example, when a blind person learns to see, perception is certainly an acquired ability. But perception cannot be the common end goal for all learning processes – that would be too restrictive. So how, then, do learning processes work in young children?

How do young children learn?

Young children in fact learn through imitation, as we described in the previous chapter. Imitation begins when an example is perceived (perceiving is the first learning process). This example is absorbed, integrated and transformed into an individual new ability. That means that the learning process in young children does not in fact take place in reverse order.

Let us take an example how young children learn to eat with a spoon:

1. First they *perceive* an example. They have often seen adults use a spoon, and they were fed with a spoon for a long time.

2. At a certain moment, children become *interested* in trying it out. They begin to connect themselves with the example of the action. For that they must be able to experience themselves as a whole with regard to their movements.
3. The first attempts will probably not be very successful. They will begin to *explore* how they can direct the movement in the right way. Eyes, hands, spoon with food, mouth and tongue, all have to be coordinated in one movement.
4. The fourth learning process consists of establishing our own relationship to the learning content. On the basis of that we *judge* whether we want to integrate or to reject the content. In this example children want to integrate the image of the action into the context of their abilities. They identify unconsciously with the image of the action as a coherent organism. The action becomes a part of themselves.
5. If that is more or less successful, it is then important not to lose the image of the action. The image of the action will have to be *renewed*, brought to life, time and again, within their own organism, by repetition.
6. Slowly the new ability *grows* and is included within the context of the other abilities such as coordination (sitting up straight, freely moving the head, judging a distance, etc.).
7. Eventually children will be able to use their ability *creatively* in other situations. It will be the basis from which they later learn to eat with a fork, or dig a hole in a sandpit.

So young children do in fact learn with the help of the seven learning processes in the usual sequence. The difference from older children is that the learning process in young children is *unconscious*. It takes the whole of their childhood for them to become conscious. Children can only manage *conscious* learning and independent memory from the age of seven.

The development of the fourth learning process

Now things begin to get exciting. On the one hand we see a development in the child from living in the action to an increasing consciousness.

The child learns to master the various levels of its constitution one by one. The direction of active learning of the child is from limbs to head; however, the incarnation into their own body moves in the opposite direction: from the head to the limbs. That process though is more or less autonomous, and falls outside the scope of this book.

What does this image show us?

Absorbing:		**Activating:**
	4. judging, integrating	
	IV. consciousness of self	
3. exploring	III. images and concepts	5. renewing
2. connecting	II. experience and encounter	6. growth
1. perceiving	I. vital forces and movements	7. creating

I. The level of vital forces

When a child imitates in a natural way there is a direct connection between the first and the seventh learning process, as suggested by Edmond Schoorel. In perceiving (the first learning process) the child opens itself to influences from the outer world; in creative activity (the seventh process) the child works from within on the environment. So both these learning processes have an element of action or vital force.

This is true even when the learning content is an insight of some sort; in this case, the concept, when taken in, acts as an influence from without on the receptive thinking; and in the seventh learning process the child's own vital force can handle the concept in a creative way. Only gradually, in the course of the first seven years, does the fourth learning process reach a stage where children can begin to make a conscious decision on this level, and reach a certain autonomy. In slightly older pre-school children the natural aptitude for imitation diminishes, and there is more room for their own deliberations before acting. From then on imitation will increasingly be guided by their consciousness.

II. The level of experience and encounter

The connection between the second and the sixth learning processes is another level that gradually becomes more conscious. Children are then able to develop a more *focused interest and empathy* for the emotional aspects of their environment (the second learning process). This interest then makes it possible for them to include themselves within that environment (the sixth learning process). As mentioned before, this attuning and including ourselves within a certain context is a musical process. Children up to seven cannot yet do this, because it requires conscious guiding on the level of experiencing and encountering the outer world.

Children learn this during the second seven-year phase, therefore, with the help of the authority of the teacher. He supplies the content, the boundaries and the direction of the way children *connect* themselves to the world (the second learning process), and how they can include themselves within the environment through this lively connection (the sixth learning process). The natural sense of connection children have with the world means that the best way to take in learning content is in an artistic form, because this allows for an inner experience and bonding. During the second seven-year phase children increasingly develop the ability to give an individual direction to their sense of connection with the world. This ability is released after puberty.

III. The level of images and concepts

In the interplay between the third and the fifth learning process, consciousness and independence gradually arise on the level of thinking and imagining. *Exploring and analysing* the learning content (the third learning process) involves absorbing thoughts and concepts, which are expressed in the environment. This knowledge is then integrated and transformed into a conscious *image* of the new ability which now has to be practised, renewed and brough to life (the fifth learning process). This process happens on the level of thinking and imagination, where the young person acquires more independence after puberty (in the third seven-year phase).

IV. The level of consciousness of self

The fourth process is related to the forces of the 'I'. The previous three levels led to the child acquiring independence. The fourth step is when the 'I' encounters itself, becomes aware of and judges itself. This process may begin around the twentieth year (the start of the fourth seven-year phase), when human beings really take responsibility for themselves and learn to act in freedom.

We have now described two paths of development. The first path led through the seven learning processes, from initial perception to new creative ability. This is how a child learns. The second path leads through the four levels of the human constitution. This is how a child develops towards consciousness and independence.

Within the limited abilities of young children, this second path can still be observed in action in the first seven years. The most important task in the first phase is inhabiting and mastering the vital forces and the motor system; in the middle phase children open up more toward their surroundings, and in older pre-school children a wakefulness develops with regard to thought and imagination. After the first seven years children achieve a first level of self-consciousness, for instance, being able to write their own name.

The fourth learning process, which connects and guides the other processes and brings them to independence, plays a central role in the development towards adulthood. It plays less of a role, however, in the first seven years where children are focused on acquiring new abilities.

Part II

The Four Types of Ether

9. The Four Types of Ether and the Four Elements

In the first part of this book we used a stream as an image for the ether world. The ether world expresses itself in time and connects past and future in an ever-changing relationship. We saw that the past mainly relates to the physical world, the evolved world. The future, however, is related to the human soul which sets in motion the processes to satisfy its desires and wishes, but also to realise spiritual endeavours and ideals. The ether world connects the motives of the soul to the physical world. Like a stream, the ether world is in constant motion, but it does maintain a certain coherence in its form. Without our ether body we would be incapable of doing anything in the physical world. We could not have a body, nor could we act creatively. For every loaf we bake, song we sing, for every movement of our arms and legs, we need our ether body.

The ether forces work in time, so we can also call it a time-body. There are lots of questions we can ask about our relationship to time, to gain insight into the nature of our own ether body, and also for example the nature of the ether body of a group of children. To work more consciously with the ether body as a pedagogical tool it is important to build up a concrete picture of it.

> *I decide I want to bake a loaf of bread. It's a pleasant job, and doing it myself I can make it just how I want. To begin, I find all the ingredients, flour, water, salt and yeast, and I set to work, mixing and kneading them all thoroughly into a big lump. I leave the dough to rise for a while. All kinds of wonderful, mostly hidden, processes transform the dough. New substances are formed, gasses bubble up. When the dough has risen enough, we can put it in the oven. There the wonderful processes continue until the bread is ready. A crispy crust has formed and within it the bread (hopefully) has the right consistency: not too dense, not too fluffy, not too dry. I am proud of it, it smells lovely and I enjoy displaying it on the table.*

When we observe this process from the point of view of the stream, we see that it is not a uniform flow through time. There is a clear beginning and a clear end, and quite a lot happens in between. The steps in this process are not interchangeable. There is a logical sequence.

To begin with there was a reason why I wanted to get to work. I wanted to do something enjoyable, wanted to eat nice bread and wanted to surprise my friends. This enthusiasm set me in motion, but in itself it was not enough to bake bread. My enthusiasm had to be directed. I had to create a concrete image of the context of the process, the ingredients and utensils I needed. All this results in a spatial form, the lump of dough, in which the activity was concentrated. But even that was not enough.

The dough itself was involved in my activity, from within. All kinds of processes took place and I could only look on from the outside. It was necessary for the right conditions to be present, like the right temperature in the oven.

The next step was placing the bread in the oven, where it became 'bread' in the real sense. It acquired a 'skin' – an inside and an outside, different from each other. The bread had become an independent body. The process was complete, it could go no further. If I left it in the oven much longer, I would ruin it.

So there were fours steps in the process of the creation of a loaf of bread:

— The endeavour, the motivation, the idea
— The spatial orientation and direction of the endeavour (the kitchen, ingredients and utensils, the bread tin)
— The inner transformation of the dough
— The completion of the process in a final form

These are four general qualities that are a part of every living process. On the whole we don't notice them because we are focused on the content of the process, in this case on making the bread, the amount of flour and water, the temperature, the lovely smells. These four phases of the process are so natural that on the whole we aren't conscious of them. But they are important. If we study them more carefully, a world of new insight opens up. In the plant and animal worlds we can observe these qualities everywhere; for example in two little birds:

In spring the male and female finch find each other. They don't spend a lot of time wondering if they really like each other; they know what to do and get to work. First they look around for a suitable place. There must be enough food around, it must be safe, the light must be right. When they find a good spot they gather materials to build a nest. This is a work of art in which little branches, bits of fluff and other useful materials are woven together into a kind of bowl. Sometimes, as a finishing touch, the birds even pick feathers from their breast to help keep the eggs warm. When this spatial form is ready the eggs are laid into it, and kept warm for a long time. There is not much else the birds can actually do to help the process that continues within the confines of the egg. A mysterious transformation of substances takes place. The body of a new bird comes into being. When it is ready and the inner force has become independent, it breaks the eggshell with its beak, and comes out. A new bird is born.

In this process we can observe the same phases we saw in bread making:

1. There is an endeavour, an urge to accomplish something.
2. The urge manifests in a physical and spatial environment, where a definite physical shape is created: the nest.
3. In this form the egg is laid, in which processes of inner transformation take place according to their own laws.
4. The process is rounded off when the body of the bird is 'ready' and has enough power to move independently.

There is, of course, a difference between birds building a nest, and a person baking bread. Their surroundings, the time of year and all that it entails move the birds to action. They can only react to this in one way: the way of finches. Each species builds its own kind of nest; a finch cannot build a crow's nest. It can only follow the instincts of the finch.

Human beings, though, can make their own choices: we choose our task, the moment and the way to do it. I can bake bread with sourdough, or yeast, or walnuts and raisins.

Both finches and humans, however, go through the four phases in their process.

In both cases there is also a connection between the soul-spiritual world and the physical world: the endeavour or urge to act does not come from matter, but expresses itself in matter. Through the four steps, the inner motivation is brought into physical realisation, increasingly clearer and more solid:

1. When I begin to move inwardly, in order to create something, warmth is produced as a by-product. Without warmth a process cannot come into physical movement. The same is true for the germination of seeds and for chemical processes. That means warmth is the physical imprint of the 'I' activity. However, warmth is an element which does not last, it can disappear. When the endeavour stagnates, warmth disappears. And with that, *time* comes into being. Time is necessary as a realm where an endeavour may be led toward physical realisation. Time is connected to warmth. Hence warmth plays a decisive role in the whole process. In different physical states of matter, warmth plays a decisive role too: whether a substance is a solid, a liquid or a gas depends on warmth.

2. An endeavour alone is not enough to get the bread made. The movement must be given direction, which it can only be achieved in a *spatial* context. It is interesting to see how the transition is made to a spatial orientation, from time to space. It can only come about through a spatial imagination, a picture. In both cases, the birds and the bread making, there is a movement from the periphery to the centre. First an area is explored in search for a suitable spot. The attention then moves toward an increasingly specific spatial form. As the space comes into being, matter is densified from the element of warmth to the airy element, which fills and connects the space.

3. The next step is really a leap. Before, there was movement from the outside to the inside; now suddenly the process reverses from the inside to the outside. Processes of transformation take place in the substance, both in the birds' eggs and in the dough. Both finch and baker can only create the outward conditions. So who (or what) takes over? To effect the transitions in the substance, another element is needed: water. Almost all chemical processes take place in the watery-element, which is denser than air. Where does the wisdom come from that binds substances to each other? It is a wisdom that works according to universal laws. If I, as a baker, know these laws, the forces can serve me. The forces cannot choose whether they want to bake a loaf of bread or not. Nevertheless they are very sensitive and attune all kinds of properties and processes to each other. This does not always happen smoothly. The odd explosion might occur! Chemical processes can be very dramatic.

4. Only the last step toward the realisation of my loaf – baking the dough – turns it into a real loaf of bread. The little bird in its egg, too, only becomes an individual organism in the last phase of the process. If all has gone well, the bread will be a physical expression of the endeavour that moved me earlier on. Something that initially was just an inner motive, I can now behold in a physical form before me. My work has been realised into matter, the earthly, solid element. It has also acquired a kind of inner life, like the little bird. The process from within has become an independent form in the outer world. A skin has been formed, and within the skin a different reality is present from the reality without. The organism has acquired its own identity within the physical world. That is the conclusion of the process, and at the same time the beginning of an independent existence. Life and death are the main protagonists in the fourth phase, along with the identity of the 'creature'. In the first phase the imprint of the spirit on the physical was in the element of warmth; in the fourth phase, the spirit imprint comes into being in the earthly element, in physical substance. This gives matter its 'imprint', its identity. When this force works deep enough, matter, too, can come to life.

Here we described how the process of creation strives toward realisation through the four elements. The four elements were known in ancient Greek civilisation, and in modern times Rudolf Steiner once again pointed out their importance. We have also described four forces that work in these four elements in an organising, structuring way. These are the four types of ether:

1. *Warmth-ether* is the force that brings a spiritual impulse or endeavour into a time-stream. We can observe warmth physically, but we cannot observe warmth-ether. However, they continually transform into each other, as with the birds. The connection between warmth-ether and warmth is the 'door' between the ether world and the world of elements.

2. *Light-ether* is the force that reveals the impulse in inner and outer images. If we light a candle in a dark room, an image of the space arises. Light reflects from objects and tells us something about their individual existence. Outer light is a physical reflection of the etheric light that works in our images and concepts. Without this gift we could not act with purpose. By isolating certain images we can give direction to a process. Air is the element that feels and fills the spaces in between.

3. *Chemical-* or *musical-ether* works in the watery element. It has the ability to connect substances, to separate them again, and to bring them

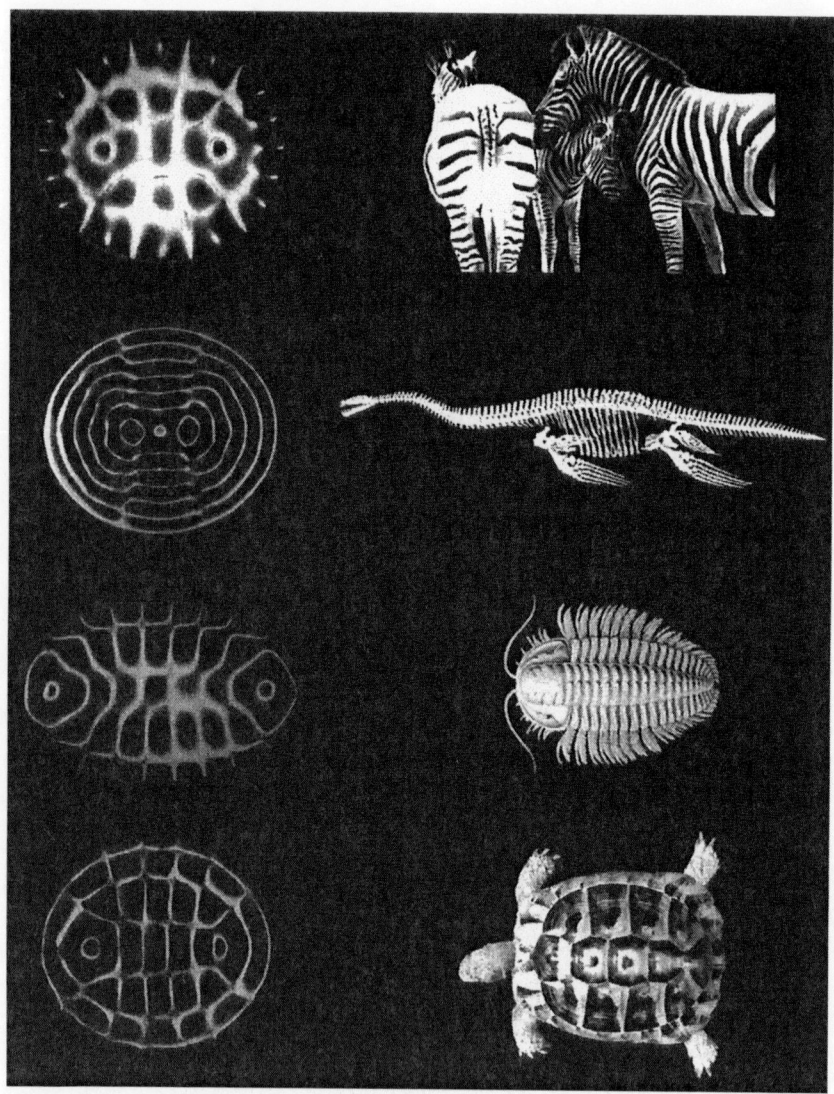

Chladni plates (from Bernd Kröplin, Welt im Tropfen)

into new manifestations. This ability is also at work in music, where individual tones are connected and separated in endless variation. When we really think, the connections between our separate thoughts are not random, and similarly the world of chemistry and music is not random. There are musical laws and chemical laws, just as strict as mathematical laws. Hence this type of ether is also known as the ether of number. The working of these forces can be made visible in a very precise way, as discovered by Ernst Florens Friedrich Chladni (1756–1827). He sprinkled fine sand onto a metal plate and drew the bow of a violin along it. The vibrations formed geometrical patterns in the sand that changed according to the frequency of the tone, the plate's form, thickness and material. Using modern instruments these forms can be analysed very accurately.

These formative forces are active in the creation of all living organisms, the organs, and the bones, which all come into being out of flowing movements. In chemical processes and in music, a very fine quality of feeling is at work. That is why music can move our feelings so strongly. In spite of the strict laws, there is endless room for playfulness and variation. Music is always in movement and can bring us too into movement from within. Tones can sound separately, perhaps causing certain tensions; water on the other hand connects and dissolves all kinds of opposites. It tries to establish connections and to create unity. This is made visible in the spherical shape water strives for when it is free from gravity, like a drop of water in the air. Water must obey gravity, unlike air. Music-ether, on the other hand, strives for lightness: music liberates from gravity.

4. *Life-ether* works in solid matter. Without the life giving force of the life-ether, solids can only fall apart. Solid matter always shows only its outside, however much we may cut it up. It remains impenetrable, incapable of any further development in time. Solid matter as such has fallen out of time. Life-ether however, has the capacity to bring solid matter to life from within and to make it serve a higher process. It imprints into solid matter an impression of the spiritual endeavour, striving for realisation. Thus 'bodies' come into existence, organisms, which are the imprint of a spiritual reality. These bodies are individual: every human body has its own 'imprint', right down to the structure of its cells. (The immune system is based on this characteristic: it is possible for the body to discern foreign substance from substances belonging to the body.) In this way, life ether brings a process to its conclusion, one could say to the point of death. This does not happen at random, like switching a ventilator on or off. We can only discern that a process has ended if we have an inner picture of the whole process; in other words: an image of the identity of the creature. So the life-ether must know the beginning of the process. It works in the process at different moments in order to realise the identity of the endeavour. Only if we have an overview of the whole process can we decide when it has come to an end. That means having a consciousness of the reason, the sense, the

identity of the process. Life ether is sometimes also called sense-ether, or word-ether, because words also contain meaning.

Anyone familiar with the work of Rudolf Steiner will recognise, in the qualities of these four phases, the qualities of the great phases of world evolution. This is not surprising. The four elements and their corresponding ether-types were created in pairs in the great world phases. They form the physical-etheric foundation of the world in which we live. All living beings, everything we create in the physical world, has to work with these four qualities. There are no other types of element or ethers (yet). There are of course the forces of sub-nature, such as electricity, magnetism and nuclear power, which fall outside the scope of this book. They are the opposites of the four ethers; the elements are placed between the workings of the ethers and the forces of sub-nature.

10. The Four Ethers in Free Play

In the previous chapter we presented an image of the four processes using the examples of bread making, and the building of a nest:

1. the endeavour, the motivation, the idea
2. the spatial orientation, the forming of an inner picture
3. the inner transformation and drama
4. the fulfilment, rounding off and purpose of the process

These are the common qualities of every living process. Usually we are not fully aware of them, because our attention prefers to stay with the specific content or the result of the process, rather than the process itself. It is like a computer: programmers have thought through every action and have worked out all the steps of these actions. If they've done it properly, we don't have to give it any further thought. It just 'works'. When we use the computer, we're only interested in the content of our email, or the colours of our photographs. This is similar to the relation between the ether forces and the human soul. We are not conscious of the forces and mechanisms we continually use. In the case of ether forces, however, we are dealing with living things, with whom we can try to establish a living and moral cooperation. The 'intelligence' crystallised in a computer is a material condensation of the spiritual wisdom carrying the world. The ether forces serve humankind selflessly and invisibly. It would be catastrophic if this were not so. But people are now ready to get to know the ether forces. The first step is to form concepts about these ether forces, to understand them. In order to observe and handle them in a pedagogical situation, we need to actively observe and explore them.

Free play

Albert (aged five) is busy making a mosaic on a table in a kindergarten I am visiting. He is an agreeable little boy, who gets along well with most of the children. He makes one mosaic after the other using coloured wooden shapes. Bernard (also aged five) is running around in the classroom. He is looking for a friend to take on an adventure. He finds Albert, tugs at him and shouts: 'Come on, let's go and find some treasure!'

Unperturbed, Albert continues working on his mosaic for a while. But finally he gives in, although he is allowed to finish his mosaic first. Bernard takes Albert and myself into a corner of the classroom. A little wooden stove is transformed into the instrument panel of an aeroplane. Bernard settles down at the controls and is off, while Albert and I are still looking for a place to sit. Albert sits down on a little wooden box and looks around dreamily. Bernard calls out: 'Look down out of the window, can you see the treasure yet?'

Albert smiles but does not answer, which earns him a reprimand from Bernard. This is repeated several times. Now Bernard becomes angry: 'Can't you see anything yet, stupid?'

Albert replies promptly: 'No, just some old shoes and socks in the water!'

He wins a short reprieve and the journey continues. Now and then Albert is scolded because he does not see anything yet. Then Bernard announces he is going to land, because he can see the treasure, down in the desert. He tells Albert to make some treasure in the meantime.

This makes Albert nervous. He picks up a little wooden swing and a doll, which happen to be lying around. But the doll does not fit into the swing; it is too big. He gets more and more agitated trying to squeeze the doll into the swing. We must have some treasure after all and we've nearly landed! Then Bernard gets up from behind his control panel.

'Come on,' he says, 'we're in the desert and we'll dig up the treasure. Have you made it yet?'

Albert hands him the crumpled doll he has somehow managed to squeeze into the swing.

'That is not treasure!' Bernard cries.

They almost come to blows. Bernard runs off, leaving us slightly perplexed. He returns a moment later, with a beautiful piece of shining gold paper. 'This is the treasure!' he announces, looking very serious. He hides the treasure under a basket, and we dig it up.

And there the game ends. Elsewhere in the classroom some children are preparing a little show, and Bernard is off again.

If for a moment we look beyond the content of the story, we can begin to see the processes underlying it.

Bernard sets the game in motion. He is running around and wants to do something exciting. For that he needs Albert and myself. Albert's mind is on other things. He is enjoying the shapes and colours of the mosaic. But he lets himself be drawn in. During the whole game the impulse comes from Bernard. It remains mysterious where this impulse comes from, but initially it expresses itself in will.

The second step in the process comes when the movement has to find a spatial orientation, a context and a focus on one particular spot. The context materialises through the imagination of a treasure hunt by plane. In this case the context remains in the imagination. Within that inner space the endeavour can now find a direction. The aeroplane, the spatial form in which the game will take place, is indicated in minimal form. A little stove is transformed into an instrument panel, the crew must find their own 'seat'.

In the third phase the drama of the game can begin. Tension begins to build: the treasure is hidden somewhere, we are on our way, high up in the air. Anything can happen. Where is the treasure? What does it look like? Will we find it? Bernard now expects some assistance from Albert, to help create some tension: *'Can you see the treasure yet?'* Albert's answer is quite a surprise: *'No, just some old shoes and socks in the water!'* In just a few words he paints a vivid picture of the situation down below. We are flying over water – a lake, a river, the sea? And it's full of flotsam and jetsam, not a good place for treasure. It is almost as if Albert paints a picture of his own ether body. The ether body often appears in the shape of the water element (a pond). Some old shoes and socks are floating around: an image of old and worn-out endeavours. Bernard will have to rack up the tension himself. He indicates that the treasure is down in the desert, and that we will dig it up. Albert is ordered to make some treasure. That is too much. He grabs some things that are lying around and squeezes them together. In a way he is still in mosaic-making mode: ordering objects in space. He cannot rise above that level. Unlike Bernard he cannot direct his imagination out of the dramatic situation of the moment.

Bernard is also the one who moves the game into its end (fourth) phase. We are going to land in the desert. He does not approve of the 'treasure' Albert has cobbled together. *'That is not a treasure!'* He even has to make the treasure himself: a piece of shiny gold paper is more satisfactory. The experience of this gold was the whole purpose of the journey. Digging it up together we seem somehow more present. We share a meaningful experience, although it does not last long. That is how it seems at least, but after several months I still remember the moment vividly; it remains active in me for quite a long time. Finding the gold is an inner experience. It gives us the satisfaction we long for in a game. So it does not make sense to continue playing the game after we've found the treasure.

Looking at it this way, it is clear that the four types of ether force are working in all free play. All kinds of questions then arise. As we can see in this example, children relate very differently to the four qualities. We can see where a child's affinities lie, and where he does not feel at home. This leads to essential questions for education.

Warmth ether

Some children have problems in the area of the warmth ether. This can go in two directions: it can be too strong or not strong enough. In the case of a weak relationship, children find it difficult to get going. It is of course important to consider the age of the child. What is the normal relationship of children to their impulses, say at one year, four years or six? If there is a real discrepancy, a lagging behind the normal development for a certain age, we should ask what might be causing it. It's a common problem: how do we help a child to get going, to join in, and to take the initiative? Motivation is a whole field of research in itself. The causes may lie within children themselves, or there may be reasons in the environment which prevent them from moving freely; the situation at home; the hollow images technology presents as examples; the mood in the classroom; a shocking experience. There may be other causes stemming from a child's constitution, a disturbance of the metabolism for example.

On the other hand there are children whose impulses are strong:

The first snow of the year has fallen and the children are allowed outside. What fun! Martin and I begin to roll a big snowball. Martin is a slightly shy, thin little boy, with light coloured hair, and an unremarkable face. He is happy to receive a bit of extra attention and joins in, although he keeps stopping because his fingers keep getting cold in the snow. But we press on. James looks on. Feet planted wide, arms wide, mouth open. He grabs handfuls of snow and chucks them at the brick wall of the school building. Patches of snow cling to it. Wonderful! I invite him to join us. He casts a pitying glance as we struggle with our puny little snowball. Not for him: too slow. After a while our snowball has grown to a respectable half a metre. It is beginning to look better. The idea of making a snowball has fresh appeal for James. He grabs some more snow and quickly rolls it over the ground. The snowball falls apart at once. This is repeated several times; he does not manage to make a snowball and gives up. He is off to pull the girls' hair; good fun too!

James is always at the centre of movement, and he draws other children along. But he has difficulty directing his movements into a context, giving them a direction he can maintain for a while. This also expresses itself within the social context of the group. All kindergarten teachers will recognise these children; hyperactivity is often involved. How can we help a child to include himself within the space, and the social space too? There is a lot more to this of course. To begin with it is important to observe these qualities and to recognise a child's strengths and difficulties.

Light ether

In the example of the treasure hunt, Bernard was at first pacing up and down impatiently. An impulse was urging him to go and do something, to have a certain experience, although it was still hidden in the darkness of his will. The idea, the motivation, which got him going, was the prospect of treasure. The second phase began when an inner space appeared for the impulse: the game takes place on board a plane (air-element). From a plane we have an overview, and we can decide later on where we want to land.

The context here is mostly in the children's imagination. The extent to which they make the imaginative space visible can vary greatly. During free play it can be surprising to see how children are right next to each other, and yet in totally different inner, imaginative spaces, hardly needing a physical interaction. At other times making an idea physically visible is the main goal of their game, and it does not progress much beyond that. When, for example, a group of children builds a great castle of blocks and planks, or when they construct a marble run with planks, the idea is physically very visible. Although it takes some imagination to construct, it is not really imaginative play.

In the case of the treasure hunters, for Bernard the construction of a beautiful plane was not important. He simply needed some space where he could create his experience. Albert, on the other hand, enjoyed the construction. Making his mosaics, endlessly ordering forms and colours, gave him great satisfaction. If this tendency in him were to increase, obsessional behaviour might arise, or phobias related to space, or the disturbance of a pure order, such as mysophobia. In autistic children too this fear for change in the environment can be very prominent. In order to judge this aspect of free play correctly, it is also necessary to take a child's age into account.

Chemical or music ether

In a next phase, the actual game begins to develop. Imagination brings everything into movement and a process of transformation begins within the physical or imaginative space that has been created. Things become exciting, go to and fro, complications arise. This can be demanding. Again and again images have to be formed of the varying relations at every moment, and also of the line leading from the past into the future. These are images of a process that arise out of a feeling for relationships. The expression of these inspirations is the chemical ether, or musical ether. As we saw in the previous chapter, chemistry and music constantly create new relationships, between substances and tones. This does not happen in a random way: both are bound to strict mathematical laws. How about the imagination of a child? That is a whole theme in itself, which would require more space than we can give it here. It is clear in any case that this is an ability capable of transforming the world, of creating new relationships. There is a certain freedom, but it is not arbitrary. On the contrary, exercising the imagination awakens the ability to inwardly sense realistic relations, and, pre-sensing, to create these. It brings about a creative relationship with the world, which can connect the inner mobility to the reality of the physical world.

This ability is badly stunted by an environment that does not allow room for imagination, such as very detailed toys, pre-printed colouring books, TV or video images.

In the example of the treasure hunt it was interesting that Albert saw an image of the water-element, with old shoes and socks floating about in it. The ether body in general, and especially the music ether, works in the water-element, as described earlier. Albert sees a realistic image of his own music-ether: he has no new impulses to move the game on. The old shoes and socks were once worn on the feet, bearers of the will.

Life or sense ether

The game came to a conclusion when the treasure was found. This experience was the half-conscious purpose of the game. By acting and diving into a process the goal could be realised physically, which was also the fulfilment of the game. It is interesting that in this fulfilment the earth element was encountered as well: the plane landed in a dry desert. The treasure itself was an earthly object too, but it was gold. The noblest and purest spirit quality is imprinted in gold. It reminds us of our own spiritual origins, which is why it gives such deep satisfaction.

The life-ether realises the experience of sense, of meaning, in substance. It imprints the identity in an organism and keeps it alive. The spirit itself does not live within the world of time and space, but its quality of 'being' is imprinted into matter as life. Therefore life is more than just the opposite of death: it is connected to the meaning or purpose of the existence of an organism in time and space. Life and death are two sides of the same coin. To know when the true point of death is reached, we have to know if the meaning of a life as a whole has been fulfilled. This insight is not only necessary in the case of living organisms, but also for a process. In children's play, for example: to understand exactly when a game has come to an end we must have insight into the meaning of its flow.

Of course a process can be terminated by an outside cause, such as when the teacher looks at the clock and signals that playtime is over. Or when another group of children wants to play on that particular spot and disrupts the game. Then the end of the game does not come from within. It is broken off abruptly and a child may need time to let go of the process.

In this aspect too children can be very different. Some give the impression that they never experience the purpose, but linger in the earlier phases. Other children seem to have a thirst for the purpose or meaning. They quickly spot the inner meaning of events, fairy tales and games, and experience them strongly.

As kindergarten teachers we can ask ourselves, how do we round off processes, with the experiences of purpose? That may give us an idea of our own relationship to the beings of the life ether.

Folk songs and ring games

Once we have become familiar with the four stages of imaginative play and the relation to the four ethers, we can find a similar pattern in folk songs and traditional ring games. Many simple folk songs have four lines or couplets and they often relate to the sequence of the four ethers. Research into the folk songs of the country in which you live can be very interesting.

Ring games too reflect the process of the four ethers. Initially there is no form, but simply the intention of doing something (as with warmth ether). Then, (reflecting the light ether), a form is shown, the coming together in a ring. Then there is movement, like one child going round the ring, often accompanied by music or singing (the chemical or musical ether). And finally there is a meeting when another child is chosen, giving purpose and meaning to the game (the life ether). Again this is a subject for further exploration, using examples from ring games in your own culture.

Questions for your own research:

The warmth ether
- What factors bring a child into movement?
- What factors support a child's engagement, which disturb it?
- What is the relationship between the children's engagement and the way I am present myself?
- What part of my own being is related to the involvement of the children?
- How do I myself relate to that area?

The light ether
- What spatial images do children create as environments for their games?

Which children tend to create physical images, and which are more imaginative?
How good are children at directing their impulses into a spatial image, also in relation to the social-spatial image of the group?
What factors are a help in that respect, which are a hindrance?
What is the relationship between my actions and attitude and this ability of the children?
How can I guide and stimulate this ability?
How do I relate to spatial images myself?
Are these images very important to me or do I see them as a useful but secondary issue?

The music ether

How do children move with and within the processes and rhythms? Do they actively engage with the stream?
Do they have the ability to develop their own imaginations in a game?
Which children flow along easily, which tend to get a bit stuck?
Which factors support or hinder the flowing-along (in imitation) and the imagination of the children?
How and in which areas do the processes appeal to me?
How am I connected to that?
Can I be open to changes when they happen?
Do I feel at ease with changes, do I enjoy them, or do they make me feel uncertain?
How is my connection to the processes related to the children?
When do they move along well with the flow, when do they find it harder?

The life ether

How do children come to an experience of purpose or meaning in their play?
Which children have easy access to these experiences, which find it more difficult?
How do children handle the end of a game?
Do the endings of their games form a meaningful highpoint and an essential part of it, or are they brought about by outside influences, unrest or distraction?
Can I observe different types of endings to games or play?
What factors support and what factors hinder the experience of meaning and a natural conclusion to play?

> How am I connected to the experience of meaning?
> How do I deal with the ends of processes?
> Am I able to sense them within the flow of a process? What happens, what do I experience? Or do I let the endings come out of external considerations, like clock time, the programme?
> Do endings have their own content or form, or are they purely a moment of cessation?
> How does my own relation to this theme relate to the way children round off?

The Land of Living Gardens

Simon was a little dreamer. He loved to watch adults working – the baker, the farmer, the woman making cheese – and he dreamt that one day he might be able to do all that work himself. He willingly helped them, and tried it all out. Sometimes travelling artists came through the town, who made a deep impression on him: a painter, some musicians and the poets. Then he dreamt that one day he himself would conjure such beautiful landscapes on a canvas, that he would touch everyone with his music, and make them happy. Or that he might encourage people with beautiful poems and exciting stories. One day a traveller arrived in the town, from a far, far country, and Simon followed him around everywhere. The stranger told stories of faraway countries and the wonderful people he had met there. Simon drank in his every word, but what thrilled him most was the story of the living gardens. Ever since he heard that story he dreamt that one day he would visit that country too.

Simon grew up into a young man. He was still full of his dream, but no one could tell him where he could find the land of the living gardens. One day he decided to go on a journey and try his luck. He thought that would be his only chance, and anyway, he did not like sitting still. Full of good spirits he set out on his way. For a long time he walked past mountains and through valleys, through forests and along rivers. He had no idea how long he had wandered around, when he grew tired and sat down on a big stone to rest. He became very sad. He thought of the long journey behind him and he doubted he would ever find this mysterious country.

Suddenly he found himself in front of a flaming gate. Before the gate stood a wonderful being that looked as if it were made of glowing flames too. Simon was startled and did not know what to do. The being looked at him and seemed to ask: 'What do you seek here, at the Flaming Gate?'

Simon told him about his journey, and his longing to see the land of the living gardens. The glowing being looked at him, and seemed pleased by the answer for the glowing seemed to increase. 'I can show you the way to the living gardens,' the being said, 'but you cannot enter there the way you are now.'

Simon jumped to his feet, his tiredness gone. 'That is wonderful!' he cried. 'I will come with you! But what do you mean, that I cannot go there as I am now? How must I change?'

Simon looked at the being and felt that through the glow, something else was radiating. It was a flaming enthusiasm, a joy he had never experienced before. It warmed him through and through, until he was as warm as he had been the moment he set off on his journey. From within, this glowing whisked him along: effortlessly he flew through the Flaming Gate.

Beyond the Flaming Gate there was a garden consisting purely of living flames. The flames seemed to carry him and speed him along even faster. The joy of the movement gave them wings. He flew on, carried along on the flames of their joy, left, right, up, down, no matter where. He saw nothing but living flames. There were places that seemed cooler and emptier. He found moments of peace there, but he never stayed for long. In these moments Simon asked himself where the journey would lead. He could fly freely, everywhere, but was there nothing else beside this garden of flames? He kept looking around to see if there was anything else.

All of a sudden he stood before a gate of light. His glowing friend was still there, now little behind him. Beside this gate, however, there was another being, made of soft and pure light. This being looked at Simon and seemed to ask: 'What do you seek, here at the Gate of Light?'

Simon told him about his journey and his joyful flight through the garden of living flames, and how he had wondered if there were nothing else to see, and that he suddenly found himself before this gate of light. The light being radiated a purity and peace that was mild and benevolent. Simon's burning desire to move subsided a little, and all of a sudden he had passed through the Gate of Light and was in another garden. The light being radiated all around and in its rays there appeared little creatures that lit up like colourful flashes of light. All kinds of colourful shapes lit up and faded again: cloudlike plants, flowers and butterflies. Everything had its place, but nothing was rigid in form. The colourful images filled the space as far as the eye could see. Simon tried to grasp all *the different images in their living connections, and the more he tried, the brighter the being shone. And so more and more images appeared and the garden seemed to expand into infinity. It was wonderful to be here. Simon could not get enough of it. And his whole being grew peaceful here and his breathing became deeper and deeper.*

Now and then he cast a glance at his glowing friend, who was still there, enjoying it all from a little distance. This garden was magnificent and beautiful, but there came a moment when it seemed that even here, something was still missing. At first Simon ignored this feeling, but it grew ever stronger. The garden of light actually appeared the same, always unity and peace. He began to long for some variation and change, but hoped the being of light would not notice. It might be offended perhaps, although Simon adored it and was grateful for what it showed him.

As these thoughts played through his mind, he suddenly stood before a third gate. It was a gate of music, and before it stood a female being that was itself filled with music. The most beautiful sounds streamed from her, always changing in their mood. Now they were cheerful, now they were solemn and serious, then melancholy, rarefied and light or majestic. Around and through this being there streamed and whirled all kinds of smaller beings. Their shapes and colours changed with the sounds of the music and they seemed to desire nothing more than to express in dancing all what they heard. The being looked at Simon and seemed to ask 'What do you seek here, at the Gate of Music?'

Simon told her about his journey, his travel through the garden of the living flames, and the garden of the flashing colours. His two friends of glowing warmth and of light still stood near, a little behind. So Simon did not say that something was missing in the garden of flames, and that the garden of light was a bit monotonous. As he spoke, the being accompanied his words with her music, and so Simon's feelings were enriched and ennobled, everything he said became music. One of the little dancing beings obviously found his story a little tedious. It did not listen to all his explanations and cried out: 'You were bored to death, weren't you? Come along, things are a bit livelier here!'

And before he knew it, he was through the Gate of Music and into a new garden, a garden differing in everything from the gardens he had seen before. The mood was filled with delightful tones, and there were little beings following the music in wavelike movements which let one form after the other appear and dissolve. They whirled round each other in great delight. You could not keep still just seeing them. Simon was swept up by a group of orange and blue beings, and it was no effort at all to follow in their flowing, streaming and whirling. More and more dancing beings appeared, larger and smaller. They seemed to be woven out of music. Simon realised that every being had its own special tone, expressing its character, and making it totally transparent. Together they created the music by dancing in ever changing combinations. The being of music appeared to encompass all these tones and inspire them time and again to new combinations.

Simon let himself be swept from one group to the other, inwardly changing with them as he went along. Slowly, however a question began to arise in him: where was his own place within this sea of sound? The question became more and more pressing. The being of music seemed to feel his question instantly. The question became music itself and formed a sound wave all around him. The music seemed to spread into all the spheres.

At last his attention was drawn to one single tone, far away in this symphony. Slowly the tone grew clearer and seemed to come closer. He felt that in some way this tone had something to do with him and he fully attuned himself to it. The tone sang in and through his whole being and he felt: this is my tone! The tone made him feel deeply happy. Now he became part of this community of music and with his tone he could sing and dance along with the others. As he danced his tone became fuller and more beautiful. He tried to make it sound in all kinds of different ways, all kinds of combinations. His tone became more and more familiar, more his own. And yet through the tone a new question sounded, increasingly urgent: where did his tone come from? The question did not leave him, and it became clear to him that he would not find the answer in the garden of music. If not here, then where?

All of a sudden he found himself before a fourth gate, the Gate of the Word. It was monumental, its forms were stern and sober. At this gate there stood a great and solemn being. It looked at Simon and seemed to ask: 'What do you seek, here at the Gate of the Word?'

Simon had to gather all his strength to be able to look the being in the eye and answer. Haltingly he told the story of his journey and his experiences in the three gardens. He sensed that in answering this being, you had to restrict yourself to the bare essentials. Each superfluous word seemed almost to hurt. So Simon soon came to the question that brought him before this gate: 'Where does my tone come from?'

The word being moved Simon's question within himself, it seemed. Simon strained to grasp its thoughts. While he tried to reach into the word being, something infinitely loving began to speak through its stern exterior, something inexpressible in outer words. It was like a homecoming.

Suddenly Simon found himself beyond the gate and in the garden of the word. His three friends of fire, light and music followed him at a distance. This garden was again totally different from the gardens he had seen before. There were rocks and beautifully formed stones and metals. It was very interesting, but seemed a bit dead at first. Between the rocks and stones, all kinds of little beings were moving to and fro, with big heads and wide-awake eyes. They were working on the stones, obviously enjoying their tasks. They seemed filled with the importance of their labour, and through them this world increasingly came to life. Their hands gave the stones meaningful shapes. Every stone seemed to speak, to convey something through its special shape. But to understand them you first had to learn to speak their language. It seemed as if the being of the word handed words to all these workers, which they made into forms with stones. Simon felt that as a guest he should help them with their work, and so he joined a little group of workers. At first they did not seem to like this very much. From the way the little beings looked at him, it was clear they thought he was too stupid for this work. And Simon had to admit that perhaps they were right. He did not understand their work very well, and he might spoil it.

Simon withdrew and did not know what to do. The great word being looked at him and understood his concern. As Simon opened himself up to him, his words began sounding in him. The words streaming to all workers from the word being, now spoke their meaning in Simon too. A new world of meaning opened up within him. Now he could help! Full of joy he returned to the group of little beings who had thought him too stupid. This time they greeted him warmly. Simon understood what he had to do, and worked alongside them on their stones. He helped many different groups and came to know and understand more and more of this garden that was full of meaning. The hard work and sober life between the stones made him more serious. But as the deeper meaning of all things spoke in him, he was filled with inner life and empathy, a wealth of feeling he would not have missed for the world.

After a while Simon remember the question he had brought into this garden. The question grew ever more urgent and he could not put it out of his mind. The being of the word noticed it and was full of attention. Simon looked at him. From the being of the word there spoke the same love and recognition he had experienced at the gate of this garden. At that moment a little being appeared at his side; it had large, friendly eyes that were very awake. The little being wanted to show him something, and he followed it through the garden. They went past all sorts of wonderful rocks and stones, past many groups of diligent workers. At long last Simon's guide stopped at the entrance to a dark cave and invited him to enter. The cave was dark but everything was visible, because the stones emanated a gentle light from within. They had the most beautiful shapes and Simon felt he was in a noble and brilliant palace, instead of a dark cave. The path descended, deeper and deeper into the rock.

After a while Simon began to worry a little. Would they find their way back? What if they couldn't? His guide seemed unperturbed and went on. Simon began to feel increasingly anxious. Finally he could not restrain himself any longer. 'Where are you taking me?' he cried out. 'I do not want to die here, deep in this rock!'

His companion stopped and looked at him with deep and friendly eyes. At that moment Simon saw a little door in the rock face. It was half open and led into a little room. His companion invited him to go in, but remained outside, as if he was not allowed to enter. At last, Simon thought, they had reached the destination of their journey. He entered the little room. There, in the middle, stood a large stone, and on it lay a small, shining pebble, radiating a softly from within, lighting up the walls. Simon assumed that a word must have been magically placed within this pebble too. He took it in his hand and tried to hear the word. This was not so easy and now he felt how tired he was, after the journey. So he sat down on the large stone and took the pebble in his hand. Simon listened intently, and after a while he did hear a word coming from within. It came closer and closer, sounding ever more familiar, until it clearly spoke out in him. Gently at first like a tender bud just opening, then slowly becoming deeper and fuller. In a flash he realised 'This is my true name!'

Sitting on the stone, Simon felt new life stream through his being. He looked all around. The forests and rivers, the mountains and valleys seemed familiar. It was the place where he had sat down in despair, after wandering around for so long. What had happened? Where were the gardens? Simon looked at the stone he was sitting on. A deep joy overcame him when he understood the form of the stone and heard the word that had been magically placed there. He felt the joy of the waves dancing in the river and heard the music singing in the water. He saw how the plants and flowers unfolded their pure forms in space, and how butterflies painted their colours onto the rays of light. And he felt again the warm glow of longing as when he had set out, the same glow with which he now longed for his home.

All these were gifts from the living gardens. He no longer saw his friends of fire, light, music and the word, but he felt their presence, their working and weaving, playing and speaking all around him. And he wanted to thank them. He saw them in his minds eye and thanked them for their wonderful gifts. A little sad now, he got up to begin his journey home. He felt something in his hand. He opened it. It was a beautiful, shining pebble. And even to this day he carries it around with him, wherever he goes.

Part III

Habits in the Education of Young Children

11. The Six Qualities

In *The Education of the Child*, Rudolf Steiner mentions six qualities of the ether body which we shall explore here. Later researchers have developed further insights. The six qualities are:

— Memory
— Temperaments
— Conscience
— Character
— Inclinations
— Habits

After the seventh year the six qualities develop a more constant and personal character. But before the seventh year the ether body has not yet ripened into a stable, individual organism. This means that these six qualities have to be provided and cared for from outside during this phase, in particular by the working of the ether body of the educators and carers. Upon reaching Class 1 readiness at about age seven, a more focused education of the six qualities becomes possible. In this part we shall look closer at one of these qualities: the habits, and shall touch briefly upon the other five.

1. Memory

Memory is the ability to condense soul-impressions, which can later be recalled into consciousness as memories. Memory forms an increasingly personal foundation in which the 'I' can recognise its own continuity. In the first seven years the memory is still very dependent on impressions from the environment, like other etheric qualities. Memory is gradually freed up in several stages and placed at the disposal of consciousness.

In very young children memory is still bound to their body, for example, a 'biological clock' that remembers daily routines. But soon they begin to recognise the people around them, especially their mother.

In a next phase of development, memory is mostly bound to physical objects. When children see an object they know, a memory is awoken of a situation connected to it.

In the middle phase of the first seven years, memory widens out to the realm of feeling. Children remember something when they experience the same mood. This is often connected to a social experience. For example, a boy sits on his grandmother's lap and suddenly he remembers in great detail how he once sat on someone else's lap, which story he was told then, what clothes he wore, where the cat was, and so on.

Only around the seventh year does the individual memory free itself to such a degree that children are able to remember anything independently from their environment. Then they can be sent to a neighbour's house to borrow something without becoming distracted along the way.

In these steps the child reflects the development of humanity as a whole.

We find memory attached to Stone Age objects, like menhirs. We find memory attached to experiences in the vast epics that were passed on in rhythmic repetition from one generation to the other, like the Finnish *Kalevala*. There are several forms of memory, related to the earth in different ways, in which individual preferences become clear. Some people remember colours more strongly, some sounds or smells. This shows that the strength of memory depends on the degree of involvement with various impressions, that is, to what extent they can be remembered later on. The more someone is interested and awake in certain experiences, the better they can be remembered.

2. Temperaments

The temperaments are formed by the interaction between the organism the child inherits from its parents, and the being of the incarnating child itself. They form an organic foundation for the mood and behaviour of the soul. That is why they only become clearly pronounced after the seventh year. The choleric, sanguine, phlegmatic and melancholic temperaments can be recognised, for example, in reactions towards the environment, or in posture and movement pattern. They form differences in the basic attitude of a person and sometimes one of the four parts has a dominant influence on the constitution. A choleric temperament in an adult indicates their 'I' is dominant; a sanguine temperament, their soul; a phlegmatic temperament, the ether body; and in the melancholic temperament the physical body. In principle each of these four qualities work in every human being, in particular, individual proportions. There are many people who do not have one clear dominant temperament.

Rudolf Steiner pointed out that in children the four temperaments are related to different parts than in adults. In a child, for example, a choleric temperament is a sign of a dominant soul, not a dominant 'I', as is the case in an adult. The sanguine temperament comes to the fore through the working of strongly fluctuating ether forces of the young child. Every child is by nature more sanguine. A phlegmatic pattern of behaviour arises out of a strong working of the physical body, which is still quite elastic and open to the working of the ether forces. A melancholic temperament in a young child is evidence of a strong working of the 'I'. Rudolf Steiner gives no indication when the transition of these relationships to the adult pattern occurs, but we may assume that this takes place around the seventh year. Various authors have different opinions on this subject, but within the context of the present book we don't have space to go any deeper. They are mentioned here as part of an overview. (Try Anschütz's *Children and Their Temperaments* for a fuller exploration of this subject.)

3. Conscience

Conscience is an organ of morality. In earlier times moral indications for life came as an imperative force from without, as rules and laws from the spiritual world. The ten commandments of Moses are an example of this. But even then, people must have had an organ for the perception of 'morality' as such. As the human being became more independent, this organ of morality developed and acquired an individual nature. Moral guidelines may of course differ from one culture to the other, even between families. It is no longer possible to lay down universal moral guidelines for behaviour, in outer forms. This would not allow room for any individual considerations. Apart from any moral instruction children receive, they must also have the ability to develop their own moral insights. This ability works within the context of values that have been formed partly through education, partly as the result of former lives. As we saw earlier, it is in the ether body where the values of soul and spirit can be absorbed and settle. The organ of morality is formed in the ether body, where attuning takes place between the earthly 'I' and the eternal, divine core (soul) of the human being. Moral intuitions come from a higher part, namely the higher 'I' or spirit self; however, they have to be attuned to guidelines for behaviour, or in other words, applied to concrete situations.

Conscience develops in several phases, through which children learn step by step to deal with their own conscience. For very young children the will of a grown up is law – and not only in the form of practical commands or things that are forbidden. Young children perceive especially the moral quality of the actions and gestures of an adult. These grow into examples the child absorbs into its being through imitation. Images from fairy tales too, provide a moral (not a moralising) environment that can have a profound influence and form a basis for the development of conscience. The young child swims in the moral content of the world that surrounds it.

4. Character

Every human being has a unique combination of qualities which are expressed in their character, and which are typical for their personality. Here too it is the ether body that contains and stores the imprint of the character. Children's character can be observed from early childhood, especially when it comes to physical expression, such as the way they move. But character develops further throughout life, through interaction with the environment. Are there certain attitudes that have become more permanent? Is someone introvert, courageous, curious, cheerful, insecure? The unique quality of a personality is expressed in their character.

5. Inclinations

The inclinations give a more permanent direction to a person's interests and preferences. In the first seven years they also, like character, become especially apparent on a physical level, such as in the inclination towards certain illnesses, or the preference for a certain food taste. But in play too, preferences and interests become apparent. One child likes playing with dolls, another likes crayons – one child loves constructing things, another loves hunting for treasure. The whole range of inclinations forms individual patterns in the child's preferences and interests, including such things as a love of music, or of technology. The inclinations are a memory for preferences, which we bring with us from a former incarnation. But they also guide children toward experiences that give them a direction in life.

6. *Habits*

Habits are the sixth quality of the ether body mentioned by Rudolf Steiner. We shall look at them in more depth in the next chapter.

12. Habits

What is a habit? In general, habits are actions and behaviour, which are repeated in a particular way. As with all qualities of the ether body, these actions are performed without having to think about them consciously. We all have many habits, most of which we may be unaware of, or may be only half-conscious. Often it is not quite clear how or where they originated. Many habits are culturally determined and were adopted from parents, or picked up at school. But there are individual habits too, in which we can recognise a person's characteristics and peculiarities.

Everyone has their own 'habit-body', a body of ingrained behaviour, which he or she can fall back on. They are a good and useful thing: if we had to think consciously at every moment before we act, we would go mad. If we hadn't learned to eat with knife and fork, we would have to look around the whole time to see how others do it. That would make it very difficult to have a relaxed conversation at the same time. This body of habits is therefore a great help. It frees up energy for more conscious behaviour. We can lean on them, and let ourselves be carried by them. We could also say that our habits become like a habitation, an etheric house of habits we can live in. To 'in-habit' is more than just to be inside a house. We feel at home where we live; we are in our own sphere of life.

The phlegmatic temperament in particular demonstrates the potential strength of these habits, but also their limitations. Our intentions from the past express themselves in habits: by repetition, these have become a part of our ether body and form a more solid foundation for our personality. Without such a permanent organism it would be hard to recognise us as individuals. On the other hand, something is missing when we live too strongly in our habits. They are a foundation for the soul and the 'I' to be able to move around in the world.

So far so good. But when we look at habits in more detail, we begin to form a more varied picture. Just try, for example, to write a description of exactly what your fingers do when you tie your shoelaces. You would probably need a whole page. It would probably give you renewed respect for a seemingly simple set of actions, because it's actually a very complicated sequence of actions in which your fingers have to work together in a very precise way. We need intelligence and concentration to perform such an action. This intelligence is partly given in the conscious image we have of a tied shoelace, and the steps needed to tie it. But the action also has a hidden aspect, which is the transition of that image to our hands. This takes place in a totally unconscious way. When the action is repeated often enough, the image will remain connected to that action unconsciously too. That is the difference between the images of actions and the images of memories, which we *can* call up consciously. We develop a particular type of memory of actions, which stores the image, and can work with it, without our conscious interference. We can always call on it, like a faithful friend, when we want to put our shoes on. Similar processes can be found for other abilities, for example learning to drive a car. Learning certain actions involve a learning process with individual stages or phases of learning.

Habits as self-evident behaviour

So is an action that has been learned the same as a habit? An action we have learned is an ability, a skill. In the case of habits it is more about behaviour, behaviour in a particular way: 'That's how it's done'. In certain situations, we behave in a certain way. That gives our behaviour consistency.

On the one hand, eating with knife and fork is an ability, a skill. On the other hand it is also a habit, because that is how we always eat, and not with chopsticks or our fingers. In the west it is our habitual way of eating. We learned the skills as children. A personal habit when eating like this may be the habit of putting cutlery on a knife rest, making little islands of our mashed potato, licking our knife after supper, or winding spaghetti round a fork instead of cutting it in little pieces.

Coming from Holland, it was a surprise to see many people in the Czech Republic use their fingers when eating pancakes. What kind of an experience does this habit give the soul? Some Czech teachers were shocked when they came to Holland and noticed that children and adults alike kept their shoes on in the house and in the classroom. The Czechs considered this to be very bad manners. When attending a seminar or conference, they bring their slippers with them. And at home everyone has their own slippers, as well as slippers for guests.

These habits say something about the folk-soul, the ether body, of the Czech and the Dutch people.

The power of habits is obvious when we try to unlearn them. Smoking is often mentioned as an example but in my view smoking isn't truly a habit. It has indeed become a half-conscious action, and has become part of the ether body, after repeated urging by the soul. But we can only call it a habit in as much as it is a way of behaving in a certain situation, such as after a meal, in a break, or as a reaction to a stressful situation. Smoking itself is, I think, more a psychosomatic habituation that leads to addiction. The word habituation is related to the word habit, but there is a clear difference here. The body grows accustomed to a daily dose of nicotine. This gives a certain sensation, which demands repetition. Often this is connected to a certain social situation (similarly for a cup of coffee, a beer or dessert). In those situations it may assume the form of a cultural custom. These sense experiences may also give psychological relaxation in moments of stress. When life is too much we may seek peace and strength in the familiar etheric home.

Where do habits originate?

A habit comes into being through repetition. Before becoming self-evident, ingrained and unconscious, the action had to be performed with the help of the consciousness, that is, directed by the soul and the 'I' of the adult. Most of our habits were learned in childhood, and are passed on by the culture of a people and a family. Where does this culture come from? In olden days habits were taught by the temples. Priests were given directions by the spiritual world about the forms that had to be laid down in a certain culture. These were often very detailed. Remnants of these instructions are preserved in the extremely detailed rules for conduct and daily life of religions such as the Jewish or Hindu culture. The habits became vehicles for the soul to develop in, when it adopted them. These 'habit-vehicles' had a deeper meaning. In different cultures very specific possibilities for development evolved.

Folk culture is a last remnant of this too. A lot of it was described and researched in the last century, often just before disappearing. In Slovakia there were five villages in the Hron valley all preserving unique customs. Certain songs for example were sung in different keys in each of the villages. Habits support the differentiation of customs and the identification with a person's own culture.

Similarly, Waldorf schools have built up their own culture. This distinguishes them from other schools. Rudolf Steiner gave an example from zoology of the octopus as an image of the head in the animal kingdom. Over the years, indications like these have often become habits. They are very useful. But we can, and should, ask whether Steiner really did want to introduce a habit with such an example.

In our time, many of these old cultural habits are disappearing. This can make us sad, but on the other hand we now have individual freedom, for example, to choose the key for a song, choose how to wear our hair, what buckle we prefer on our belt, and what examples we choose in zoology. This search for personal identity and lifestyles has become heavily commercialised.

Habits are increasingly becoming an expression of the individual, though this requires a bit of effort. This is apparent when children grow up and the house of habits they inherited from their parents begins to feel oppressive. Then a lot of things are turned upside down, before a newly renovated habit house rises from the dust.

Then why adopt this house of habits from the parents in the first place? A child arrives on earth without a house of habits. Stefan Leber writes about a state of etheric homelessness. Everything is new all the time, must be observed anew, experienced and thought through. That is very exciting but also quite exhausting. So it is important that a child should receive a good house of habits from its parents. After all, if we don't have a house to begin with, we can't renovate it later.

Because the soul and the 'I' of the child have not yet developed (see Chapter 1), children are dependent on the examples of behaviour they see and experience in their environment. They learn habits by imitation. In the first seven years the child builds up a foundation with the help of its environment, which will have reached a certain stability at Class 1 readiness. Edmond Schoorel is quite justified in saying that habits connect us to the past, to examples of behaviour that have become familiar. Imitation connects us to the future: something new is learned.

We can address a school child, age seven or more, more consciously. School is the time when we can build up a child's house of habits in a quite conscious and focused way, not through imitation, but through the authority of the teacher. What a child absorbs through imitation and authority can then be further built up and be renovated as they become an adult. In our time, the individuality of human beings has become so strong that we are more and more able to build up our own houses of habits. In the following chapters we shall study habits in more depth, as well as the possibilities for adults to build our houses of habits into instruments for pedagogy.

Questions for your own research

Can I describe some important habits of myself, my culture, my family?
Can I observe differences between habits and skills?
Are there certain skills, which sometimes appear in the guise of habits?
Are there habits I have developed myself?
Are there habits I have unlearned?
How did I manage to do that in both cases?

13. Habits and Our Connection to the World

In the previous chapter we explored the concept and nature of habits, and we had a look at several habits. There are many different habits, and it is perhaps useful to create some order. If we see habits as a form of cultural behaviour in certain situations, then we can differentiate between them according their content.

Habits of the physical body

In the first place, there are habits mainly related to the physical world and our own body. How do we behave in relation to that area? What habits have we been taught? How do we eat, wash, dress, how do we clean our living space, look after plants and animals, how do we travel, and so forth?

These kinds of habits are most important in the first three years of a child's life, although they remain important throughout the whole seven-year phase. We acquire our habits in this life; we do not bring them with us from former lives. This means a newborn baby does not yet have a house of habits. It reacts to every new impression with its whole being. That is exhausting, so a baby needs a lot of sleep. The rhythm of waking and sleeping is the first exercise in habit forming, whereby waking up is related to feeding. In this phase of life the most fundamental habits are learned: not only the rhythm itself, but also *how* the child feeds, falls asleep, wakes up – suddenly or gradually, full of attention, or stressed. This is the basis of future personality. In recent years the importance of this phase is increasingly being recognised, for example through research into the quality of bonding.

Of all our habits, the habits in the physical body remain the most unconscious. On the whole we do not think about whether we put our left sock on first or our right, what position we sleep in, whether we break an egg on the edge of the pan or with a knife, eat slowly or in a rush, how often and when we touch our nose. We become conscious of a habit when something in our environment changes, for example when we move house, and we keep expecting a light switch in the place where it was in the old house. Or when we are on a bus and try to look in the rear-view mirror as if we were driving our car. These examples are funny because they are so trivial. But when it comes to habits and the ether body in general, it is the details that matter. Here the smallest, down to earth details can become interesting. They can teach us a lot about ourselves, things we'd sometimes rather not acknowledge (especially when it comes to bodily habits). However, young children also imitate habits we would like to hide from ourselves. They copy us unquestioningly. We may even feel caught out sometimes. But they offer an opportunity to gain a good insight in ourselves.

Physical habits provide us with a basis for our connection to the physical world and to our own body. Through all these habits a kind of basic attitude may become apparent, for example, care and attention or messiness, decisiveness or tentativeness, well formed or half-baked ideas. In these attitudes, a moral value comes to expression too. When young children receive a good house of habits, it will be a great and lifelong gift for them. That is why attention, joy, respect for materials, for their own physical body and for sense-impressions in general are of vital importance to them.

Habits of the soul

A second area is habits that relate to the soul, to social situations and relations, and also to thoughts, moods and motives. How do we usually handle these? How do we greet each other, for instance? In the United States people behave in a less formal way, and in the Far East people behave in a more circumspect way than in Europe. How do we talk and listen to each other? How do children enter the classroom? How is seating at a table decided? Do we hold hands when saying grace? Who does the clearing up after playtime? How do we decide whose turn it is in a ring game? How do we sing for the birthday child? How do parents enter the classroom? Habits give social situations a predictable form, allowing the inner life of the soul to be communicated in a comprehensible way. We need a few basic agreements, in order to be able to vary them to a certain degree.

This type of habit is a little more conscious than the habits related to the physical and bodily world. We are more present in them, even though they are based on certain accepted patterns. We become quite conscious of them when we meet people with different soul habits. How do we attune these habits to each other? That is a whole theme in itself. On the whole we try to adopt the habits of our host or hostess, but of course there are difficulties and they have to be resolved on a more conscious level.

Habits of thought

The life of the soul is supported by the habits of thinking, feeling and will. What habits of thought can I recognise in myself? What do I think when my daughter comes home too late, when a piece of junk mail comes through the letterbox, or when a boy of four years old spills his porridge all over himself?

To begin with, young children need clarity. Because their own ether body has not fully developed yet, they cannot appeal to their own individual thinking. They absorb habits from their environment through imitation. That includes the 'everyday' thoughts of adults – not just the thoughts which are actually thought or spoken, but the thoughts which speak out of the behaviour they see. How does the teacher react to an unexpected visitor? How does she react to a restless child? What subsequent thoughts speak through that behaviour?

When a teacher shakes the hand of a child as it comes into the classroom, her gesture communicates that she sees the child as an individual, not merely as something to be looked after.

Our politicians give us bad examples in certain habits of thought. All too often they thoughtlessly regurgitate the party line. This thinking, calcified into habit, becomes a hollow phrase. They have not personally lived through and wrestled with it.

It depends on the personal, individual presence whether a habit of thought is filled with life or remains an empty husk. In order to prevent children from becoming fixed in their habits of thought, it is good to leave them space for their own imagination and to give them examples of playful exchange, joy, open attention for the world around them, which continues to surprise and amaze.

Habits of feeling

A range of habits is found too for our moods and emotional judgments. How do we react when something makes us cheerful, or disappointed? What facial expressions do we usually display when we experience those feelings? Do we actually know these things about ourselves? We could explore this in much more depth. We know more or less how the people around us react. It has its advantages to know how to interpret children's moods from their facial expressions. At the same time it can be very restrictive if we navigate too much by the image we have of someone's habits, and fix them to that with our expectations. It can become stifling. 'O dear, there's William, he will probably start messing around again.' Children especially are in constant development, and their behaviour can change rapidly. Moreover, the way adults look at them has a deep effect on children; they strongly react to the image we have of them.

They may oblige and begin to display the behaviour we expect from them, or resolutely refuse to do so. Positive and open attention, for example in a child study session, can work miracles. Living attention for the child is of vital importance. The negative caricature of this are the conventions, the fixed expectations of certain behaviour that prevent an open and living encounter. We must protect our children from these. So where is the dividing line between these, and the regular habits which children do need? Pedagogical habits too can begin to work like conventions and stifle social life. The many rules and regulations that are forced upon a school from outside can be stifling too, and undermine the responsibility of the teacher. Again, the question of whether we ourselves live with habits is crucial, and how those habits are attuned to a particular situation.

Habits of action

A third group of habits of the soul are the habits related to action. In a sense all habits are actions – they are behaviour after all. The quality of behaviour is judged by how meaningful it is within a social context. Our habits, our customs allow us to move and act in a meaningful way in our environment. It is important to have a sense of the whole action as an overview. After playtime, we naturally clear away our toys, or we help a younger child to dress. We grind the wheat to flour, the flour is made into dough and we knead it, put it in the oven and after a while the buns come out. Then we wash up everything and when the buns have cooled off we put them on the table. An image, an overview of the whole process, gives each separate action within it a meaning, so that it does not remain an isolated, random action. This image of the whole can enthuse us for the action.

Habits that have lost their meaningful context can disturb or become a hindrance. Unsuitable habits can cause strife and misery.

In an environment with habits of crude language, without patience, attention and openness, or with a craving for violent impressions from the media, and careless behaviour, more accidents are likely to happen than when a good and meaningful house of habits has been built up.

The habits of action can degenerate into caricature too and become *routine actions*. Without a genuine interest in the meaning of our actions as part of a whole, actions become machine-like, simply performing their limited function. Many actions in modern society do not rise above this level, both at work and at home. This is one of the causes of depression and absenteeism. The will may also express its frustration in senseless violence, where the action becomes a goal in itself. Routine is not the same as regularity. Actions descend into mere routine when we no longer attach inner meaning them. The living inner relationship to an action is lost.

It is obvious that children should be spared such bad examples in their education. Children can experience and learn meaningful behaviour, by seeing it in their environment and imitating it joyfully.

We have discussed three caricatures of habits in the life of soul: the hollow phrase, convention and routine. Rudolf Steiner pointed to these three caricatures as the causes for chaos in our society.* Well established habits can create a good foundation for the culture of the future. Between the ages of three and five children are more open to absorbing good social habits.

Habits of the spirit

A third area is the habits which form our relation to the spirit. These come to expression for instance in a verse or grace at mealtime, a song after playtime, a story, a prayer before bed. Lighting a candle can also acquire meaning in this way. The content of these habits forms our relation to the spiritual world. How do we relate to it? How do we behave in this realm? What spiritual content do we want to give our children? In what forms can we experience this content and bring it to life? In kindergarten, the slightly older children in particular need such habits and customs. They form the foundation on which a child may later find their own conscious relationship to the spirit.

---

* *Social Issues*, lecture of March 17, 1920.

In our times this relationship to the spirit is in crisis too. On the one hand a living relationship to the spirit seems to have become impossible for many. It is hard to imagine a reality other that the immediately perceptible one. On the other hand this has led to cultural forms becoming calcified and rigid.

How can we build and maintain a living relationship with the spiritual world?

To achieve this we first have to strengthen our powers of concentration in our thinking, which can then free itself from outer perception. Secondly we must put this strengthened thinking to the service of images and inspirations from the spiritual world. This means strengthening our will, but also opening ourselves up to a spiritual reality expressing itself in its own meaningful coherence, the way a plant seed reveals itself according to its own being, not influenced by the observer's subjectivity.

The foundation for this ability can be started early in childhood. Children can absorb the qualities of concentration and respect by imitating adult examples. Openness and reverence for a higher content, perhaps at first not fully comprehended, can be formed in childhood in particular. We do not have to explain the image of the Madonna, the deeper meaning of the grace at the table or a fairy tale to young children in kindergarten. These images have an integrity of their own which conveys itself to children, even if they may not be able to verbalise or explain their content. In fact, children are still unconsciously connected to the spiritual reality in all phenomena. When we provide an environment of reverence and inner peace where children can have these experiences, then as adults they will be able consciously to develop this attitude, for example in meditation and prayer.

Spiritual habits such as a prayer are purposeful forms through which a higher reality can communicate itself. They are not meant to remain totally unconscious. Repetition and regularity give extra strength to these forms, which allows a spiritual reality to come to life within them in a better way. It makes a real difference if we say a prayer such as the Lord's Prayer occasionally, whether in need, or daily for twenty years without personal motive. In meditation too, repetition has a strengthening and enlivening effect. Rudolf Steiner offered a number of very valuable meditations, which we can work on over a long period. This creates forms in our ether body, which can form a little temple, to which we can return time and again. In education in particular, these meditations can be of great significance and support.

How can we prevent these habits from becoming automatic, and how can we form them into a vessel for spiritual substance? How do we build a living relationship to the spiritual world, as a basis for working with children? It is clear that this theme can be explored much further.

In the following chapters we shall consider how habits can be used by teachers as educational tools.

Questions for your own research

Physical habits

What habits do I have on the physical level?
What physical habits do the children have, does the group have?
How do I evaluate these from a pedagogical point of view?
Which of these habits have I developed consciously?
Which of these habits would I like to transform?
How do I relate to the physical world?
Does something of a fundamental attitude show in that behaviour?

Soul habits

What habits do I have in thinking, feeling and will?
What habits in thinking, feeling and will do I see in the children?
How do I evaluate these from a pedagogical point of view?
Which of these habits did I develop consciously?
Which of these habits would I like to transform?
How do I behave in thinking, feeling and will?
Does something of a fundamental attitude show in that behaviour?

Spiritual habits

What spiritual habits do I have?
What spiritual habits do the children have, does the group have?
How do I evaluate these from a pedagogical point of view?
Which of these habits did I develop consciously?
Which of these habits would I like to transform?
How do I behave towards the spiritual world?
Does something of a fundamental attitude show in that behaviour?

Can I discern comparable fundamental attitudes in the different areas of habits? Or are there differences?
What would I like to change in this fundamental attitude?

14. Habits as a Medium for Education

In the previous chapters we have explored the nature of habits, where they come from, and how different habits connect us to the world in different ways. In this chapter we shall look at some aspects of dealing with habits in education.

The habit-body of the group

A group in a kindergarten has a body of habits, in the same way that a culture or a family has a body of habits. One difference is that the habits in the kindergarten group are not inherited, but have to be established and maintained consciously. The teacher uses her own ether body to direct this process and to give it substance. For the kindergarten group, she embodies a kind of folk spirit. It is very interesting to study how such a group organism comes to life and how it can be supported in different ways. Earlier we mentioned several aspects of this process. Children on the whole find their way quickly into such a house of habits. It is also amazing to see how quickly they can switch from one organism of habits to another. At home there are probably other habits than in the classroom, and different ones again at their grandparents' house. Children don't need a lot of explanation. If the house of habits is well built and clearly defined, switching to the habits of the kindergarten is usually quite easy. It helps of course if the basic attitudes are more or less the same. When a child is used to coarse language at home, watching a lot of television, or a fixation on the intellect, the transition may be more difficult. This can raise the question of whether the parents are really prepared to enter the 'cultural stream' of a Waldorf school.

Interestingly, the problem does not always lie in the specific content of the group habits. It is quite possible to integrate a Muslim child into a kindergarten group, and spend some time painting henna-red hands at Eid al-Fitr. Inner attitude is the key phrase: a positive attention and respect for human beings, and an interest in children's development. A

Jewish-Arab Waldorf kindergarten in Israel, for example, has adopted customs from both Jewish and Arab culture.

The habit-body of the educator

We all have our own habit-body. If we have to educate young children, this acquires a new meaning. Children are dependent on our ether body. This is true for parents and teachers alike. A teacher has to manage an even greater changeover than a parent. It is not just a matter of moving from one house of habits to the other. Our own ether body acquires another meaning.

Having my own family taught me a lot in that respect. I had to reconsider all kinds of habits I could permit myself as a bachelor. I had to become an example and my actions acquired an educational meaning: no more listening to the radio at mealtimes, and always beginning mealtimes with a grace, perhaps washing my socks a bit more often, or telling the children a story at bedtime. So I couldn't be on the phone the whole time, organising things. Only when the children are in bed and the house is quiet is there peace to meditate. There are habits we may have to suppress, others must be newly acquired. It can be a bit unsettling, but it can also be stimulating. It is an opportunity to spring clean our house of habits, and allow for new experiences. And above all, everyday life all of a sudden becomes much more interesting. There is an added meaning to it. Ordinary things acquire a religious meaning and begin to communicate themselves to us in a different way.

Moving between work and family we have to switch time and again. For kindergarten teachers that is very important. There may be a difference, but we cannot cut ourselves in two. The two worlds, home and kindergarten, will always have a certain influence on each other. If we have problems at home, how do we free ourselves from those in the classroom? How do we deal with those contrasts? Do we bring our work home and sing a song before our meal, even if we live on our own? Or do we bring our home into the school and answer the phone at any moment in the classroom too?

A certain difference is healthy of course; home life has a different quality from school life. A teachers' staff meeting is different again. But the differences should not be too big. If we nourish our habits at home, they will give us a basis for healthy habits in the classroom too. Looking after our ether body at home makes sure it is in a good condition for using it in the classroom: sensible bed times, a certain regularity, completing things, a structure for our personal religious life; these are all fairly obvious.

The Pedagogical Law in self-education

Rudolf Steiner's Pedagogical Law applies not only to the education of children, but also to adult self-education. As we have seen, it states that the medium or tool for educating a part of the human being is always the part immediately 'above' that one. Children up to seven are building up their physical body, so as teacher we use our ether body as a pedagogical tool. The ether body is the part of the human being just 'above' the physical body. If, as their teacher, we want to educate our *own* ether body, we do that using our soul, the part just above the ether body. How does that relate to the habits?

Habits originate in the life of soul. If I like wearing slippers at home, I will wear them often, until it becomes a habit, until I do not think about it any more. If I enjoy coffee or tea after a meal, and I repeat that often enough, this behaviour will settle into my ether body. In this way a foundation of habits is formed which, however, also reflects back on the soul. If we get irritated quickly or are easily discouraged, if we are very neat, or cheerful, these attitudes can settle into our ether body too. We grow accustomed to reacting to certain situations with these attitudes. We can begin to see how far-reaching a spiritual training is that aims to develop the ether body into an instrument for education. Certain ingrained, fundamental attitudes and moods may not be suitable for the environment young children need. That is one reason why not everybody is suitable for this work, although of course nobody is perfect for it either. If, for example, we decide to work with young children because we are very insecure, and feel secure among children, then that is only justified if we are prepared to do something about our insecurity. Children need clarity and look to us for safety and security.

Making the ether body suitable for use as an educational tool means, above all, being prepared and able to restrain unsuitable habits and to behave according to what the children need at a particular moment. We have to make our ether body subservient to the children's needs. Instead of indulging our own habits, we must sense what the children need in a particular situation. For most of us that is a lifelong but wonderful task. Developing our ether body into a suitable tool means becoming active in several ways in our life of habits. And of course, no one is perfect. Our own limitations can be very frustrating, but we must not despair. Children actually prefer someone who is not quite perfect, but is prepared to work on themselves. That too serves as an example for them. Working with a group of children is a privilege, because it is an enormous help for self-development. The children accompany us on our path. Each and every group, teacher included, is a karmic community on a path where all of them can develop. It is a magnificent gift in life.

The power of habits

> There was the situation of a Waldorf kindergarten group within a state kindergarten in the Czech Republic. This gave rise to tensions because each had a totally different culture of habits. The management of the school did not always understand the habits and customs of Waldorf education, and the management were often quite restricted by a plethora of regulations. This meant that teachers of the Waldorf kindergarten group within the state kindergarten were sometimes forced into situations they did not agree with.
>
> In all kindergartens in the Czech Republic, children have a rest after lunch. Sometimes the children from the Waldorf kindergarten went to another classroom for their rest or for lunch, for example, if a lot of children were ill and the management wanted to save on heating. The other (state) classroom, however, was quite different. Teachers shouted at the children and the children were quite restless. So the Waldorf teachers were worried that the children of the state school might swamp their children with their restlessness. They decided to bring certain customs of their rest-time into the state schoolroom. They brought several wooden frames making a tent of pink cloth for the youngest children (from 2 ½ years), as they were used to in their own classroom. The state teachers and children too were very interested. They were very pleased to adopt this wonderful habit. The upshot was that all children slept peacefully.
>
> The enforced communal lunch had a similar effect. The Waldorf teachers had made up their minds to at least say grace in silence. At first there was turmoil and shouting. One of the state

schoolteachers shouted something to them, just when they were saying the grace in silence. But she caught herself in mid-sentence and walked away. After a while she came back, this time in a very different mood. Since that time she always whispered when she came into the Waldorf kindergarten during rest-time. And someone even heard her tell a fairy tale to her children a week later. The ether body was quietly at work.

It is a real task for teachers and carers of young children to 'inhabit' the organism of their own habits ever more firmly and consciously. That builds up a power, which is often underestimated or even denigrated. The example above shows that it can be a powerful force, radiating through its surroundings without the necessity of intellectual explanations. It is important to stay true to it.

The whole in the parts

The theme of habits leads us to our everyday behaviour. To work with behaviour more consciously in an educational situation, we have to be more awake in a realm where we are normally asleep. We have to engage our will strongly here to achieve anything. The challenge of kicking a smoking habit shows that clearly. To change or form something in our ether body, we need greater strength than when we change our soul, because the ether body is a level deeper and offers more resistance. On the other hand, anything our 'I' achieves in the ether body remains our 'spiritual property', even beyond the boundaries of this life. As an exercise in changing something in our etheric, Rudolf Steiner suggested changing just one letter in our handwriting.

Habits cannot just be erased. Edmond Schoorel in his book, *The First Seven Years* mentions two possibilities to change a habit: to overlay it with another habit, or to restrain it, to ignore it. In both cases the 'imprint' in the ether body is weakened.

And of course, we do not have to change everything at once. Within the ether body everything is connected, interrelated. If we change one aspect, it will have an effect on the whole organism. And *vice-versa* the whole organism is present in each of its parts. If we study one of our habits carefully, we find qualities in it that say something about the state of our whole ether body.

A kindergarten teacher, when she examined her habits, came to the conclusion that her ether body had a rushed quality. She had a habit of leaving home at the last moment and arriving at school in a restless mood. She resolved to walk to school calmly and full of attention for her surroundings every day, leaving home a quarter of an hour earlier. Not only did she notice many new things along the way, but her peaceful attitude had an effect on her attitude towards the children, and also her own family.

Little things make all the difference. After all, we gain more by making such a small step, carried by our 'I' than if we live a life of thoughtless routine. In the following chapter I will give a practical example of how we can practise and work with habits.

Questions for your own research

Transforming old habits and behaviour

What habits or attitudes would I like to transform from an educational point of view?

How would I do that? Do I have any experience doing that? I may, for example, have a tendency to be irritable, disappointed, impatient, messy, melancholy, indecisive, and this expresses itself in all sorts of habits.

What do I do when a certain verse, say a table grace, becomes too much of a routine?

Adopting new habits

What habits or attitudes would I like to develop or strengthen from an educational point of view?

How would I do that? Do I have any experience doing that? For example, developing a more cheerful disposition, attention to detail, a warm empathy towards the children, regularity and consistency, a fundamental trust in the spiritual world, etc.

Have I ever developed these kinds of attitudes or behaviour in the past? How did I do that?

What else would I like to learn in this context?

Pedagogical behaviour

Am I able to react to a situation with suitable behaviour and actions?

> Can I remember any instances of that?
> What habitual attitudes do I have in store, at the ready in my educational 'toolkit'?
> Can I hold back my own preferences and habits when necessary?
> Can I name any examples of that?

15. A Practical Example of Individual Research

In this chapter we shall look at an example of how as a teacher we can find our own way into training and transforming our habits in a practical way. This is just one example, there are many different ways. Everyone can do their own research. It is not necessary to read many books or to know a lot of anthroposophical jargon. This is how we worked on this subject in the Czech kindergarten teachers' workshops for two years. Researching habits can be a way of gaining real insight into our ether body in relation to young children.

We shall follow four steps.

1. *Forming an image*

First we can form an *image* of a number of our most important habits, beginning perhaps with habits in the classroom, but also habits outside which continue in the classroom. What habits can we describe?

Each teacher then chose one habit, which we explored further with a number of questions.

Here we shall take one teacher's example of lighting a candle before the meal in kindergarten.

1. What is your habit, in what forms does it express itself? Which realm does it belong to?
The habit consists of always lighting a candle before lunch. The children are all sitting at the table in their usual places, and so am I. The candle is in the middle of the table. It is usually wax-coloured and always placed in a special candleholder with a wide base. Around it there are sometimes a few little twigs and beautiful stones. We renew the candle when it totally burns down. We light the candle with a match from a beautifully decorated double matchbox. The unused matches are in the upper box, the used ones go in the lower box, and so you are never left holding a burnt-out match. When the children are nice and quiet I stand up, and bend

over the table to pick up the box of matches. I take a match from the upper box and light it. Sometimes I check from the corner of my eye that the children are really quiet. I extend my arm with the match to the candle in middle of the table. I light it and extinguish the match by blowing it out. Then I put the used match in the lower box and put the matchbox back in its place. Then I sit down and say grace. I think it is a spiritual habit, although it has a social aspect too.

2. Where does the habit come from? Who instigated it?
It is impossible to tell who initiated this habit. The candleholder has been on the table for two years now; every season we make a new matchbox and decorate it. I adopted this habit.

3. What is the time-body of the habit like? How often does it appear? How long has it been alive for?
This habit has been with us from the beginning of the kindergarten, twelve years ago. It happens every day and takes about 40 seconds, from the moment we are all ready, until I sit down again and say grace.

4. What is the educational value of this habit and of this particular form?
The purpose is a moment of reflection. The candle is a living flame demanding attention. The flame is like an apparition of the spirit. The atmosphere becomes more alive. The children feel that too, they find this little flame very interesting. Lighting the candle creates a moment of reflection, and respect for the meal.

We use beeswax candles when we can, because they have such a wonderful smell. The little stones and twigs emphasise the special quality of the candle. It is clearly not a toy or a tool. That is a meaningful experience too.

5. Has the habit remained the same during its existence, or have there been changes?
The actions have remained the same. The matchboxes, the candles and the little stones have changed, the teacher too.

6. How are the children connected to the habit?
The children know what will happen. They expect the candle to

be lit and know all the details of the actions. They often notice when the matchbox has changed. They are not always as quiet as I would like.

7. How am I myself connected to this habit?
I have adopted this habit, but I am committed to it. I still find it an exciting moment. I want to create a mood of attentiveness, which is very sensitive. I need keep to my attention on the action, but I also need to be aware of the children inwardly. I don't always manage it as I would like, for example when the children are restless. Then I am disappointed.

2. Making observations

Once we have built up a picture of the habit like this, we can begin to observe it over a period of time, with the help of a special diary. We choose six or so details we want to focus on, perhaps with the help of the above questions. In this example questions 6 and 7 are particularly important, because the children were restless sometimes and the teacher wanted to find out more about that. At the end of a day we can write down some brief observations in a diary. The diary could look something like this:

Points of observation	Monday	Tuesday	Wednesday	Thursday	Friday
1. Appearance					
2. Duration and experience of the time					
3. Was the educational purpose obvious?					
4. Did anything change?					
5. How were the children present?					
6. How was my own relationship to it?					

Example of a diary

After a period of time, when we have observed the habit at least seven times, we can study our notes and compare them with the picture we began with. In the example of the candle, the teacher kept her diary for more than a month.

3. *Processing our observations*

We can now begin to ask more questions. We evaluate the habit, as well as our own relationship to it:

— How did the habit manifest itself?
    Has anything changed?
    Does it serve its educational purpose?
— How did the habit become manifest in time?
    Is there a clear relationship to time (duration, moment, passage, development)?
— How do the children relate to the habit?
    How are they present in it?
    Is there a change, a development in their presence?
    Does their relationship match the educational purpose of the habit?
— How am I connected to the habit?
    Can I see a development in that relationship?
    Are there tensions?
    Can I make the educational purpose visible, inwardly and outwardly?
    Can I observe a direction, an individuality in my 'house of habits'?

4. *Formulating new plans and goals*

Helped by insights gained in this way we can start afresh: make a change or introduce a new habit, which we can then observe again with the help of a diary. We can also set further learning-goals for ourselves. The kindergarten teacher in our example realised that when lighting the candle she was actually quite tense and insecure. She practised different ways of being present: where do we focus our attention? On the match and the candle, on the children around us, on our own inner mood? Or are we caught up in our own expectations and tension? It was clear that the teacher herself was easily distracted and looked around her a lot, which was also related to her temperament. She set herself the goal to be more present out of a mood of inner trust. The actual form of the habit was not that important in this case. It had a strong form and fulfilled its purpose. This may be different in other cases.

The following example shows that sometimes a change of form can work wonders.

> One of the teachers in the workshop wanted to say grace before family meals. This caused a lot of bickering between her daughters of 6 and 11. They quarrelled about other things too: who could light the candle, who could help themselves to food first. So she initiated a new form of this habit. One girl would light the candle and say grace, while the other helped herself to food first. They alternated from one day to another. It worked immediately and it still does.

Lighting the candle before lunch was also an exciting moment in a particular kindergarten in Slovakia. What caused this unrest? We identified two main causes.

> The first cause had to do with outer forms. The children sat at a very long table. That makes it hard to experience yourself as a group with a common centre. You see this elongated form in the limbs, where it supports movement in the outer world. A group at a long table quickly splits into sub-groups of children sitting next to or opposite each other.
>
> As many as half the children could not see the candle because there was a pot plant in the way. They decided to use a round table, and that made a big difference. The candle was visible for all and there was a common centre. In a bigger group you could use two round tables if necessary.
>
> The second cause lay with the teacher herself. How do you deal with restlessness at the table? Do you insist on silence and wait with a serious expression until they are all quiet, before saying grace? Or do you admonish restless children? Either way you risk losing them. When you sit still with a serious face and let the children carry on, they do not sense a boundary in you. They cannot relate to your presence very well. But you do expect them

to consciously maintain a boundary. That is too much perhaps for very young children. In the other approach you run the risk of being drawn into the children's restlessness. If you get angry, the mood you wanted to create vanishes.

There are no hard and fast rules (or answers), but there is a particular strategy you can try. Here the teacher could address the situation by connecting to the conversation of the children, and guiding it in the direction she wants. When a few boisterous boys challenge her by talking about trains she might say, 'Dear train drivers and conductors, where are you travelling to?'

After their answers she could continue, 'Wonderful, we shall just leave the train at the station for now, so the conductors can have their lunch, and after lunch they can continue their journey.'

This way you relate to the children's reality, they feel acknowledged, and not rejected. This allows them to go along in your direction.

A kindergarten teacher must be present in her habits on several levels at the same time. Studying a habit means taking a certain distance. On the other hand, leading a group of children with her ether body demands intense engagement. That is why it helps to write down observations afterwards. A new insight can also help us sense certain tendencies quicker, in the moment, and deal with them better.

This kind of self-education can be quite a struggle, but it also makes life much more interesting. There are deep secrets hidden in our everyday habits, waiting to reveal themselves if we search for them earnestly.

16. Designing, Conveying, Maintaining

We saw how activities can become habits when we repeat them often enough and they become second nature. We don't have to think about them any more. When we have reached that stage, the 'image of the action' of the habit has come to life within the ether body. We continually create etheric forms in this way; we could also think of them as beings. Our etheric body is filled with such etheric beings of all kinds. We can become acquainted with these etheric beings, the being of a habit for instance, by asking it questions. For example:

— What do you look like? (image of appearance)
— How old are you? (image of time)
— Who are you, what is your name? (image of meaning: in a name the purpose or meaning is verbalised)

These questions lead to an *image* of the habit. In the previous chapter we asked questions like these while trying to describe the habit we were researching. They help us find out something about the habit itself.

Three exercises in relation to habits

If as kindergarten teachers we want to explore our *relation* to a habit, we can ask it further questions:

1. Where do you come from?
2. How did you come to be in this ring?
3. What do you need to be able to live here?

These questions lead to our relationship with the habit acquiring a new dimension.

1. Where do you come from?
If we ask where a habit comes from, we enquire into the person who

created it. Habits are often adopted from someone else, but some habits we perhaps designed and created by ourselves. But in both cases the teacher has received them and learned them.

If we adopt an existing habit, it does not demand a lot from our own creative inspiration. This is not necessarily bad, sometimes it can be good to adopt a habit that lives in a group already. Here we shall explore what happens if we create a new habit. How do we go about that?

How do we get the inspiration for a new habit? Some people sit down and try to form a clear inner picture. Others receive inspiration while working with the children, or doing something totally different. In any case there must be an inner *question*. That question provides the attraction, the suction as it were, for the inspiration.

Two factors increase our chance of receiving a better answer: the *clarity* of our question, and the *urgency* of our question.

We have seen these qualities before, in Chapter 6 on the goldfinches. The clearer the image of the group, the situation, the pre-conditions, our own goals and wishes, the greater the chance of finding an image of a suitable habit. So it is important to prepare that inner picture very well. We offer this inner image up to the spiritual world as a vessel. The answer may come in the form of an image, an inspiration that suits the situation.

Isn't that amazing? We receive an answer from a world of wisdom and artistic sensibility, a world where the inner essence of the different aspects of the situation are blended into a meaningful whole, into a suitable and fruitful image. Here we encounter the ether world in its conscious aspect as the *contents of thought*. When we discussed the seven life processes in Chapter 8, we indicated that the ether world is active in two different directions: within the organism as the life processes, and in consciousness as the learning processes. But it is one and the same ether body! The wisdom working in organic processes is the same wisdom we open ourselves up to in active thinking. The more we strengthen our thinking, by concentration and forming of images in a focused way, the more we can connect to this wisdom-filled stream of life. In other words we can practise receiving good inspirations.

2. How did you come to be in this ring?

When we have designed a new activity, we need a second step to bring the activity to life as a habit within the group of children or the family: the activity has to be *conveyed*. How do we do that?

This is a totally different process. In designing and planning the activity it was enough to have an inner picture of the group of children; now, in conveying the new activity, the children must be present physically. But they do not know the activity yet. The teacher has an image of an activity – a song, a game – and has to find a way to convey that to the children. If the children are very young, then imitation is the obvious way. An interaction develops between teacher and children, they enter into a kind of conversation from different starting points.

This demands a totally different way of being present, compared to the process of designing the activity. The teacher demonstrates something, observes how the children receive it, adjusts it if necessary and repeats it, over and over again, perhaps more quickly.

At first she clearly leads the process, but as the new activity settles in, she can hold back a little and create space for what arises in the ring. So *conveying* has a time aspect, it is a developing process.

The relationship at the beginning: the teacher has a mental image of the new activity, which the children do not know yet – she is in charge, the centre of attention, the children are dependent on her and imitate her.

The relationship at the end: the children know the activity too and are increasingly able to perform it. A habit-form arises in the group with a life of its own. The teacher is increasingly peripheral, creating the right conditions, harmonising, correcting.

Teaching a new activity is a process of transition from a central to a more peripheral role for the teacher. Finding a balance between these two in every moment is an art in itself.

Here the ether body acts as a mediator. Every moment it creates new relationships, attuning inner and outer, central and peripheral, form and chaos, movement and stillness. The teacher can be less awake now than when designing the activity, because she alternates between being active within the stream and being outside it. While designing she was on her own; when conveying she is more connected to the children. She cannot maintain such a conscious distance as when she was creating the activity.

3. *What do you need to be able to live here?*
Once an activity has been learned and the children in a group or family know it, a third step is needed to make sure the activity is maintained and does not deteriorate. We have to care for the activity, to tend it. How can we do that?

How do we form the activity into a habit with a life of its own, which *stays alive* when the initial excitement and playfulness of learning are over? Then the teacher does not just provide a form, but withdraws to a certain extent, to allow room for the independent dynamic that begins to live in the group. Her presence becomes, as we've already seen, peripheral: carrying, enveloping, feeding and harmonising. She reaches the end of this withdrawing gesture when the children begin the song spontaneously, without her example, or sit down at table in their own place, or do the ring time game once more by themselves during free playtime. Then the teacher has become a part of the environment, where the children feel safe.

Maintaining and *caring for* are both necessary to keep the habit alive. Maintaining has a more central gesture: the teacher makes sure that all goes well and guides the game she as she wants it. Caring, tending, is a more peripheral quality, an enveloping, nourishing attitude.

People differ widely of course. Some have a more 'central' maintaining attitude, others a more peripheral and nourishing attitude. It seems natural to associate these qualities with the masculine and the feminine. Working with young children, the peripheral attitude is more appropriate on the whole. This means that the teacher may have to sacrifice part of her central attitude as an adult, to be able to connect fully with the stream of life. If she can achieve this, she in turn will also be carried by the stream.

Community of life

An activity that has settled into a habit has incarnated deeply into the organism of teacher and children. It is no longer a matter of flashes of inspiration, nor a matter of playful activity, now within us, now without. The teacher must be wholly present now, and connect with the stream. Here the ether body is apparent in a more organic way. The teacher and her ether forces have merged as it were with the etheric organism of the group of children. She cannot just step out of it. This bond, this connection, lives more and more on an unconscious level. The habits have a power of their own now. The teacher has to carry and feed this force with her own ether body but she is nourished too by this communal organism. Problems may arise if the activity does not quite come down to earth, or the teacher is not fully behind it with her will. If she has an inner resistance against a deeper connection, against regularity and tranquillity, against a peripheral, nourishing attitude to life, she will struggle inwardly, which can cost a lot of energy.

Individual paths of schooling

Everyone's ether body is different. In particular, everyone has their own preferences and limitation with regard to the three tasks: *creating*, *conveying* and *maintaining*. What are the consequences for how we care for our own etheric forces?

The blackbird
For some, the process of creating is swift and good fun, while maintaining is perhaps a bit of a trial. Their ether body is more inclined toward consciousness, to the content. For them it may be more of an effort to incarnate into life processes and find rhythm and regularity there. When this attitude is extreme they will flutter around like birds, or only sing beautiful songs like a blackbird on a roof, without finding deeper peace in their own organism.

The cow
Other teachers may find the process of creating more difficult. They struggle desperately to make up a song, and in the end prefer someone else's song. But they love being among the children, calmly sitting among them with some embroidery, now and then guiding them gently in their play. They feel at home in familiar activities, the smell of the bread, the lovely soapy water, the daily walk, the pumpkin soup at Martinmas, the pine smell of the advent wreath. For young children this mood, this attitude, is very pleasant and nourishing.

There is a danger that this teacher can become a bit too comfortable in her own metabolism, too earthbound. Imperturbably the cow chews and ruminates the contents of her four stomachs. Her gaze is inward, her warmth radiates into her surroundings.

The cat
Particular skills are needed for the task of conveying. The ability to attune is important, as well as a playfulness, a feeling for interaction with the children. Here the ether body takes on the role of mediator between the qualities of the other two tasks, creating and maintaining. The magic word here is rhythm. Finding a new balance in every

moment, in the constantly changing relationships in a group, is a real art. By nature children love going along with a game. For the teacher it means continually sensing different *boundaries*, between rest and movement, communal and individual, concentrating and releasing. This is the art of breathing in the activity. Young children have not yet built up their own rhythmic system and are dependent on the rhythms in their surroundings to help them build up their own organism.

Teachers with a feeling for this are like kittens playing with their siblings. They come up with wonderful playful movements: challenges, mock attacks, hiding, running away, funny attitudes, arching their back, tail up, or a quick sideways jump, withdrawing or playful biting, an endless variety. And always with faultless timing, the right action at the right time.

This attitude becomes extreme when the frolics never stop and there is no time for children or teacher to gather themselves, either in the force of their metabolism or in the inner concentration of consciousness. It can become an addiction to relating for its own sake.

Care of the ether forces of the teacher

It is extremely important for teachers of young children to care for their own etheric forces. Because everyone's ether body is so different, this care and maintenance are very individual matters. Depending on the nature of the teacher's ether body, there are different approaches. Various artistic exercises can be helpful. What is tiring for one person may be refreshing for another.

It is wonderful to listen to a blackbird, singing its song to the heavens. Or does heaven sing through the bird? Frolicking kittens and dolphins cheer us up; resting near a warm cow can be soothing and help regain our strength. As human beings we unite all these qualities in an individual balance.

Part IV

The Group as Etheric Organism

17. The Size of the Group

To recap, we are trying to discover the reality of the etheric, in particular in our work with young children, because Steiner's Pedagogical Law indicates that the ether body of the teacher acts as the main 'educator' of children up to seven years old. We cannot perceive the etheric world with our eyes; it is supersensory, but we can observe its working, its effects.

The influence of the ether world is so all-encompassing that in a strange way we are not aware of it. One example is the group. We don't really see a 'group' as such. We see a number of children together in a certain space, but that does not make them a group. If we put twenty-five young children together in one room to begin a new class, that would be painfully obvious. And twenty-five toddlers would be a different story altogether – quite a task. So what is present in a group of children that have been together for longer? What is a group, really? What qualities can we observe in a group, and how do we work with them? These are some of the questions we shall look at.

We have already discovered several qualities of groups: a spatial aspect (a number of children together); a time aspect (a group develops only after a while); and an age aspect (what are the unique factors and qualities in forming a group of children up to seven?)

The size of a group

When does a group come into being as a unity? That in itself is an interesting question which we explored in our workshops for kindergarten teachers. Everyone agreed in their feeling as to how many children form a group. One child is not a group of course. But two children? Or three, four or five? It is interesting to sense what happens in groups with these numbers. Most teachers agreed that seven was the minimum number and that a group really came to life with more than ten children. Why is that? What arises in a group that size that is different from a group with fewer children? It is not something visible, but we can perceive it. A kind of inner world comes into being between the children, supporting and connecting them. Something begins to flow and weave, to live a life of its own, something that was not present before. A teacher can work with that, but it demands a different attitude than a group with fewer children.

We can also ask another question. Can a group be infinitely large, or do groups have an upper limit too? Just imagine: a group of fifty children, or a hundred. What would happen? It is obvious that what flows and weaves in a group of ten children or more can be lost when there are too many. On the whole the teachers agreed on an upper limit too. There were some differences, but they felt the upper limit was about 23 to 25 children, although some felt it was 18. What happens then? When that number is exceeded, the coherence is lost. There is too much of a 'mass' to be carried along in the flow and weave of the group. Of course this limit is related to other factors too: the space, the age, and how many children need special attention. Nevertheless, just the quantities tell us something.

Threefold image of appearance

Purely based on the number of children in the group, a threefold image appears.

With a low number of children, the attention is more individual. The children are more busy by themselves. The teacher has to spread her attention equally, and to guide each child individually.

With a number of between ten and twenty-five a communal life arises in the group. It is harder to give each child individual attention. The teacher has to react more to the rhythmic movements of the group as a whole.

More than twenty-five children in a group is impossible. A single teacher cannot take forty young children to the toilet, wash their hands, and do a ring time game. Children who cannot keep up will be left out, breaking the flow. They start to do other things, messing around or whining, because they lose sight of the whole. The teacher can no longer envelop them with her ether body and bring them along.

It is clear that a small group inclines more towards the individual quality of the world of soul. The middle group can flow along with the etheric movements of the group organism, and a larger group threatens to fall apart, like a physical substance that can no longer be worked through inwardly. The individual differences are lost; the children are in danger of becoming objects in a mass and they protest against that.

Pedagogic approaches to group size
Both small and large groups are more exhausting for a teacher in a Waldorf kindergarten, striving to share an etheric organism with the children. She has to tune in to a different wavelength suitable for groups of a different size. Other methods of education sometimes have a different emphasis, although there is rarely a totally one-sided approach. In Montessori schools for instance, attention is focused mainly on the individual child.

What pedagogical attitude do we need for a smaller group? We will focus more on each child individually, on their own path of learning and play. We support their own journey of discovery, help them to overcome hindrances, and give new indications and ideas.

It is very interesting that the size of a group suggests different pedagogical approaches and methods. With a large group, it is practically impossible to penetrate with our own inner reality. It will take a great deal of energy and we run the risk of burnout. What attitude does a large group demand? We cannot do much else than treating the children as objects. When a real inner relation is impossible, the only thing left is to order, 'Sit down! Don't touch! Be quiet!' That was the attitude to the children in the old Dutch *Bewaarschool* (literally, 'the school for storing'). I came across this attitude several times in state kindergartens in Eastern Europe. Sometimes the teachers made life easy for themselves. I saw teachers smoking and drinking coffee in a room next door while one of them was on duty with the children. Or children were dumped in front of the television or a video. If they grew restless, the teachers shouted from next door to keep them quiet. These are extreme examples of course; there are many teachers who do their work with a very warm heart. But often the main aim is to keep the children quiet, not causing any trouble. An inspector for kindergartens in Slovakia once asked me, 'Our main problem is how to keep the children quiet, do you have any ideas?'

The Waldorf kindergarten and the group organism

Waldorf kindergartens focus on the group organism. There will, of course, be moments when children receive individual attention, or play on their own, for example during free play, which is an important part of the programme. There has to be a certain outer discipline and order. But our approach works mainly from the ether body of the group. The chapters on the stream, the flow, made this difference to other approaches clear. We can look at the same activities from an 'object perspective' or a 'process perspective'. The approach focusing on the group is well suited to the level of development of toddlers and kindergarten children. Children are carried by the whole, their individuality does not need to be emphasised too much. They can progress in their own way within this safe stream.

This approach has another important advantage. Because the ether body of young children up until seven has not ripened into an individual organism, they need their environment to provide this etheric cover. When the teacher works in her group out of an etheric orientation, this creates the best circumstance for a conscious relation on the basis of *example* and *imitation* This is harder both in a small and in a large group. Through group activities, all kinds of clear rhythms and habits are built up which give the group organism its own strength. This strength carries the children along during the day. There are many things they do not have to think about: they can enter into the familiar forms and activities full of joy. Imitation works not only from the teacher to the children, but also between the children themselves. They imitate each other, and the stream in which they live together. So there are several processes that form a group into an organism with its own structured inner life. A tremendous constructive and harmonising force works from this. Children still forming their own ether body can be carried and supported by it.

Working with a group we need to do spatial-communal activities, and also to follow a communal, rhythmical stream through time. The activities in space are embedded in the stream of time. The fact that there are more and more children who have difficulty being part of the organic life of a group shows that etheric forces are under pressure in our culture. These children do need extra attention, if possible not instead of the group but as a part of the group. Individual attention is no substitute for the special nourishing and constructive influence of a group organism on children.

Size of the group and the phases of childhood

The relationship between the quality of a group and its size also depends on age. Forming a group with very young children is harder. They constantly need individual physical attention and are not yet able to be part of the group because they do not have the physical maturity. Here the ether body of the teacher mainly cares for the child and its surroundings. But on a soul level the child does merge fully with its environment. The ether body has not yet become so individualised, which means the child does not yet experience a clear divide between inner and outer world.

School children on the other hand are already so independent that they do not automatically flow along in the etheric stream. They can make their own decisions, and the teacher can appeal to that capacity. Physically they can enter into an organic cohesion with the whole. They can dress and undress by themselves and take part in communal activities. Their ether body is so independent that they can stick to a certain task. All this means that the power to imitate is diminishing. The authority of the teacher comes in its place, and the child gratefully accepts it. That is why from Class 1, a teacher can manage larger groups, although there may be some children with special needs who require extra care and attention.

Children of kindergarten age fall in between these two. The group organism provides great support to children in kindergarten in the forming of their own individual organism. The older children in kindergarten are developing towards the condition of the school child. The group provides a safe environment where a child is supported. The rhythms, customs, role patterns and rules give it clear boundaries and support, so the child can find its own way. Compared to a toddler, who needs more care and attention, a kindergarten child is able to take part in a more individual way. The group helps the child on its way to independence.

So age is another factor in the search for the ideal size of a group. It becomes possible to have larger groups as the children grow more independent. After puberty new questions arise with regard to the ideal size of groups.

Another question is the problem of children with special needs. Children with a social problem, a motor dysfunction or a developmental disadvantage need extra attention. But it is important for them, too, to form part of a group. It may be a way to soften their isolation, or even to overcome it.

The teacher and the size of the group

The size of a group points to certain qualities of the group. When evaluating the size of groups there may be differences between individual teachers. This depends in part on their etheric constitution. For some, a group of twenty children may be too much, but another can manage twenty-eight. You cannot argue about this because these differences are determined by the constitution. Experience can, of course, also be a factor. But it is a mistake to determine group size on purely bureaucratic or financial considerations. We need an education system that proceeds from a very sober assessment of the actual constitutional abilities of individual teachers and children.

For teachers there is also the question of which part of their constitution they work from. This is not only a matter of individual differences in constitution. One teacher has more energy than another, some are perhaps more sensitive or better with practical, technical matters. These differences lead to a different emphasis in the teacher's approach.

But we are also dealing with a certain *world-view* as the basis for our educational approach. Consciously or unconsciously, this world-view creates expectations in our work. If these expectations do not correspond with the reality of a certain group of children, disappointments and frustrations may arise. If we prefer to approach children individually, then it can be difficult to work with the image of a group and to engage with that image as a reality. But the image, the ideal of working with a group, has to be kept in perspective, too.

> *In a Waldorf kindergarten they always said a beautiful grace at the table. The children knew the grace and expected to hear it before lunch. During the grace they were usually quiet. By the end of the afternoon, a number of children would have left. At about 3 pm, the small remaining group would have a snack, some fruit and a cup of tea or juice. For that occasion the teachers wanted to say the same grace as they had used before lunch. The same children who knew the grace and always listened to it attentively at lunch, now became restless. It did not work. It was not the same group*

that it was before. The teachers had to use a simpler grace, which appealed to the children to join in individually. This then worked well.

The size of the group made the difference here, it called for a different approach. If we cling to our expectation of approaching the children as a group, we may find there are moments when it just does not work. These situations require a creative reaction to the children's reality. In this case that reality was influenced by the size of the group.

Questions for your own research
When do the three qualities become apparent in my group? Do I make a clear choice in those instances? In what do I observe the organism of the group? Is that organism strong and has it developed in a differentiated way? Can I consciously apply or hold back the three approaches?

18. Inner and Outer Space of the Group Organism

The size of a group is one aspect of the appearance of a group organism. In a lively and inwardly-formed group an organism has come into being with its own inner and outer world. How do we perceive that organism? Entering a kindergarten as a visitor you just see a number of children together in a space. They move about, doing all kinds of things. But does that mean you have perceived the group? The fact that you are not able to join in their naturally unfolding activities shows you do not know the organism of the group yet. To learn to know the organism you have to read, as it were, between the lines of your separate observations.

If you do, you notice for instance that the children slowly drop their free play, when the teacher sings a certain song. If you spend a whole week in the group you would begin notice many of these connections. As the week goes by they become more and more apparent, and you can join in. When you don't have to think about the different activities anymore, and you flow along in the stream naturally, your ether body has become attuned to that of the group. They mutually strengthen each other.

So it becomes apparent that the etheric organism of a group has a quite differentiated inner world. This needs a certain protection and care. All kinds of factors can influence it in a supportive or in a disturbing way. At the centre of all this is the teacher. The quality of the group organism depends on the way she herself relates to her own ether body. Exploring this relation can lead to interesting discoveries, for example during free play time.

Looked at from the outside, the children are playing by themselves or in little groups during free play time. So from a physical point of view the picture is quite differentiated. We do not see an outer communality in the group, as for example in a ring time activity. It is interesting to observe how a teacher is present in this. Is she sitting on a chair, or walking about, looking at what the children do, intervening or giving suggestions here and there?

Or is she doing something herself, which takes up all her attention? Ironing, sowing, mending or spinning, for example? Many teachers will know the strange phenomenon that when they are fully involved in something practical, the children around them will also be fully involved in *their* play. If the teacher moves around, looking at the activities of the children, a totally different mood arises, which the children tune in to.

We can see that in families too. In a family where the mother constantly gives her children attention and comments on what they are doing, there is a different atmosphere compared with a family where the mother is more centred in herself and her own tasks. In the first case the mood will be more restless. Sometimes children have to make an effort to establish and secure an inner space for themselves. In the second instance this is not necessary. Often the children will come to their mother, keen to help, or they feel secure in their own play when the mother does something familiar, like cooking or washing.

In developmental psychology a phenomenon has been described that also points to an invisible connection, without being able to give a scientific explanation for it. Mildred Parten, for instance, mentions *parallel play*. This can be observed in young children playing alongside one another. On the one hand they are fully involved in what they do. On the other hand they also observe what the other child is doing and unconsciously absorb things from each other without communicating. The ether body works in a connecting way; there is not such a clear spatial boundary as in physical objects. Without direct interaction, the two children somehow influence one another.*

Of course it is not always possible to draw a clear line between being relatively self-contained and fully present with the children. Even while peeling apples we keep half an eye on them. But they are clearly distinct attitudes illustrating again the differences in educational approach. In the 'mass' approach to education of just looking after a large group of

---

* Rupert Sheldrake observed this phenomenon and called it the 'morphic field'. These are force fields that surround, for example, a species of animal. When you teach one particular animal something, the other individuals of the species will be able to learn the same thing quicker. The morphic field seems to retain the new experience, and the other animals in the same field have a connection to this. From an entirely different perspective, Gustav Jung arrived at the concept of synchronicity, the synchronic occurrence of phenomena in different places, such as if you want to phone someone and that very moment the other person just happens to phone you first. Inventions (such as the printing press) are made at the same time in different places.

children, life in the inner space of the organism is lacking. There is no connection to the ether sphere. The soul of the adult teacher is fully focused on the physical presence of the children. Equally, we must ask what happens to the etheric realm when individual attention for children is the main focus.

The skin of the group

Part of the care and maintenance of the group as an organism is the way we look after the 'skin' of the group. The skin is an incredible organ. It is not just a boundary, or an encasing. A skin is permeable from both sides, but it is not simply open like a window. The skin filters and regulates warmth, moisture, air and light, for example. It also attunes these different elements to each other: when the organism becomes too warm for instance, moisture (sweat) is secreted, to lower the temperature. This is performed by the sweat glands which cooperate in a very subtle way with the warmth-organism. When a physical object penetrates the skin, it is encapsulated, or driven out by an accumulation of moisture (pus).

On the *outside* of the skin there is an attuning to the conditions of the outer world. It is amazing how well the skin protects against harmful substances, such as paint, petrol and cement. Human beings can handle all kinds of materials and wash them off afterwards, without these having penetrated their body too deeply. If the skin could not do this, these substances would do a lot of damage within the organism. So the outside of the skin has the task on the one hand to physically repel, but on the other, it also absorbs influences from the outside, for instance balm or oil that heals the organism.

Another function of the skin is perception. The skin makes us aware of other spatial objects through the sense of touch. It tells us something about the qualities on the surface of these spatial objects: hard, soft, warm, cold, moist, dry, rough, smooth, etc. Through the skin we can also perceive qualities in the atmosphere: warmth, humidity, sound, light. The skin can even change colour through exposure to light. In a way the skin is one great organ of sense perception.

The *inside* of the skin is attuned to the inner world. There are connections to the organism as a whole through the liquid substances (blood, sweat, etc.) and the nerves. There is sebaceous fat and there are tissue structures that build up the skin and help with isolation (because of course the inner world must stay within). Within the skin different laws hold sway from without, and they would be disturbed and broken if the protective skin should fall away. The immune system uses the skin to protect and maintain the special qualities of the inner world.

What can we say about the skin of a group? Is it just as ingenious and differentiated? How do we perceive it?

On the whole the skin of a group is most in evidence when there is a meeting or a confrontation with an alien element. For example when a group from a kindergarten meets another group of children. That makes us more conscious of the group we belong to. And also when a foreign element comes into the group, like an administrator who wants the teacher to sign a letter. What happens then? The skin is touched. How do the children react? Do they become restless? The children are easily distracted by the visitor, causing the inner attuning, the harmony of the group to dissolve. How do we deal with that?

What happens depends on the teacher. After all, her ether body is the centre of the group. She could go up to the administrator and discuss the matter at the door. She may then sit down at a table to sign the letter. What happens to the children then? How do they react?

Another option is hissing to the visitor that they are not welcome, that this really is the wrong moment. How would the children react then? A third possibility is hanging a sign on the door saying, *Please do not disturb during school hours.* No confrontation, no problem.

The outer world is always present somewhere and affects the group organism in many ways. The teacher may feel that administrator could come in again at any moment. Other classes may have their break time and run around outside the building or have a noisy lesson next door while the kindergarten has its rest time.

These issues arise with parents too. To what extent are they allowed into the classroom? Is there some sort of agreement? Some parents like to have a chat when they come and pick up their children. If the children are all picked up at the same time, chatting with one parent means the teacher cannot talk to the others. If the parents do not all come at the same time, the teacher may not want to talk to them when there are still children in the classroom.

I worked on this theme with the teachers of two kindergartens. There were several new teachers who could not understand why we could not receive parents in our classroom and have a lengthy conversation with the children present. Or why it might be better to switch off a mobile phone in the classroom. The younger generation especially is very used to being constantly available on their mobiles. But something is lost. These quick and superficial 'zappy' contacts dilute our engagement with what we are doing, in other words, with our own ether body. And more importantly we are talking to someone who is not physically present. How does that affect the children when they imitate it?

How do we discuss these issues with people? Do we just state our principles?

That could lead into an authoritarian or preaching attitude, which calls up resistance, achieving the opposite of what we hoped for. That was exactly what happened when the director of a kindergarten tried to discuss this with her staff. A different approach was called for.

> *It's possible to work from a teacher's experience, without much explanation. In this case we did a number of movement exercises to experience the realm of the ether world for ourselves. It went very well. There was a tangible, intimate atmosphere of presence. That can have a deep effect, right into your physical body. People feel more comfortable, relaxed, they begin to breathe deeper, or to yawn. Right at that moment, fate lent a hand: the phone rang. The ring tone cut through our being, we were shocked, and it was almost painful. And all of a sudden it was clear what effect that has. There was no further need to explain anything.*

Of course there is the question of how to translate our ideal to practical everyday situations. How do we deal with parents? The group of teachers I mentioned also came up with several practical solutions.

There are different options and we have to remain flexible to a point. But it is possible to stick to certain principles and make them work in practice. Considering the group as an organism with an inner world, we can ask everyone to respect this. Another approach is that here too, we can introduce certain habits suited to the group organism. So we will not have to explain everything again and again in every situation, and solve the ensuing problems. As we have seen, habits are a part of the ether body. In this case the ether body of the group can extend into the surroundings. The group takes up part of the surroundings into its own habit-organism. The environment becomes part of it. This etheric attuning to the environment forms an important enveloping sheath for the group. It can strengthen the ether forces of the organism. I did the above movement exercises with parents too. They worked very well. An attuning and understanding are certainly possible. We constantly have to look for possibilities to foster understanding and respect for the reality of the group organism.

Let us return to the image of the skin, and the way the skin mediates between inner and outer world, and serves as an image for the relationship between the group organism and its surroundings.

— *Encapsulating:* We take the visitor to one side and talk outside the life of the group.
— *Driving out:* The visitor meets a closed community and can't relate to the communal process. The teacher remains totally involved in the group process. The visitor senses: this is not a good moment.
— *Rejecting:* The sign on the door makes it clear that the visitor cannot come in. In the extreme it means locking the door.
— *Balm:* What could work like a fragrant oil or balm on the skin of a group? A supportive parents evening? A sympathetic organism of habits in and around the group? A fresh, clean classroom and school buildings, cleaned with fresh smelling natural detergents? A lovely garden round the school?

Welcoming visitors

The skin regulates the relationship between the organism and the outer world. It absorbs the effects of the outer world into its own rhythms and life conditions. Many different solutions can be found for all these issues. When a visit is announced beforehand, it can be absorbed into the organism better.

We can also conserve the etheric force of the group when we turn the visit into an occasion for the whole group, with a role for the children. This is possible with an unannounced visit, but that demands more improvisation of the teacher. The children need time to adjust, although that also depends on who the visitor is. A little mouse creeping in under the door will instantly catch their attention.

But on the whole a visit that is announced is more successful. Some visitors are very welcome after all! We certainly won't hang a sign on the door for Father Christmas or St Nicholas saying, *Please do not disturb during school hours..* A trainee teacher may also be very welcome. They will just have to fit into the group organism and find their place in it.

The teacher's ether body once again

It is important what arrangements we make. But again, a lot depends on the ether body of the teacher. How does she relate to her own ether body? If this relation is strong and well maintained then it provides enormous strength to handle tricky situations, precisely because the ether body works on a deeper level than the conscious soul. Here are two examples.

> *A Dutch kindergarten teacher had found her own way in this. Having been distracted several times by visitors, and become irritated, which took her even further away from the group, she decided not to let it happen again. Whenever there was an unannounced visitor she remained where she was, in the ether sphere of the group. The visitor experienced this as a very strong power, a closed shell they had to respect. Obviously the teacher was in different realm, where the visitor could not communicate with her, to quickly arrange something practical for example. When you are strongly present in your ether body then the soul (of the visitor, for instance) will have to adjust to that. That is one way of solving the situation.*

> *If we have a strong connection to the children, then it is possible that we can maintain it if outside influences force us to react. A Czech kindergarten teacher experienced this. Her Waldorf kindergarten was within a state school. The relationship was not such that she could ask the director to come back later. She told us how the director came into the classroom with a rather technical question. She was in the middle of a ring game with the children. She took the director into the corridor and talked to her, with the door open. The amazing thing was that the children just continued with their ring game. They kept their etheric group connection with each other and with the teacher. Again we are left with the question, who did that?*

So it is possible to come to some general principles, as described above. On the other hand we must judge every situation afresh and each situation may demand an individual, unique response. And a good thing too!

> **Questions for your own research**
>
> In what do I observe the organism of the group?
> Is it strong, differentiated?
> How am I present during free play?
> What influence does that have on the children?
> How do I care for the skin of the group organism?
> What rules and habits are there in relation to the environment of the group?
> How do I care for the skin of the group organism with the quality of my presence?
> What relationship do the parents have with the group organism?
> Are the parents understanding? Have we established agreements and habits with regard to their connection to the kindergarten?
> How do I deal with unexpected visitors?
> How do I deal with visitors that I do expect?

19. The Development of the Child Within the Group Organism

In the previous two chapters we looked at the group organism from the perspective of the size of the group and from the perspective of the dynamics between an inner and an outer world. In this chapter we shall look at the development of the child in relation to the group organism.

We have seen that a group is more than just a number of individual children. We can sense an inner cohesion, as if a group were a living organism. The organic coherence of invisible relations takes time to develop. That is the next aspect in the development of the cohesion of the group: *time*.. What is it that takes place in a group after a certain time?

Two boundaries in time

As with the size of a group, we can observe two boundaries. The first boundary is the very first moment when cohesion in a group of children begins to appear. How do we perceive that? How long does it take? How long does the group take in the morning to come to life?

The question arises every year in a kindergarten when a number of older children have left and new children have joined. It takes time before a strong cohesion forms. It can be interesting to see that children who stay often begin to behave differently and take on roles of the children who have left. These roles too, seem inherent to the forming of a group. That is another aspect we can research. The children stream through the inner structure of the group organism and can fulfil various roles within it.

At the other end of the spectrum is a group form that is maintained for a long time. For example when a celebration or a fairy tale takes a long time. What happens then? What time limits become apparent in such a situation? How long does it take before tension and engagement begin to drop: ten minutes, half an hour, an hour? And why? How do we deal with moments like these? Rhythm is one of the most important aids when caring for the time flow, as we saw in previous chapters.

The upper limit in time can be sensed in a family remaining together in the same constellation for a long time. What does it feel like when the children are still at home at thirty, plodding along in the same old habits? What has been lost in such a case? Or in case of a job: why do some professional partnerships split up after years of success? It is a feeling they have outlived something. All the possibilities of a particular etheric group form have been exhausted, and instead of revitalising, they become tiresome. Things begin to drag, habits become a burden. This feeling can also arise within a shorter time span, for example when a ring time game is repeated too often. There must be some change, some renewal now and again, otherwise the communal form goes stale. The chapters on the types of ether showed that processes in time also go through certain general phases.

Development of a group and of an individual

The composition of a kindergarten group changes time and again and has to re-constitute itself over and over again. Because of these constant changes it is not easy to experience the upper time limits of a group. But it is possible to sense at the end of the school year: we cannot go on like this much longer. It actually has to do with the development of the children who outgrow the kindergarten.

So we have to distinguish between the development of the group as an organism, and the development of the children themselves. Their relation to the group changes because they grow older. The life span of a group depends on the engagement of its members. If their engagement with the group is lost then the group organism cannot come to life anymore. But there is a difference. The group as such lives on within the kindergarten, although there are new children streaming through it. The constant factor in all this is the teacher who maintains the group organism with her ether body.

The ether body of the group is strengthened to the degree to which the children can tune into it with their ether body. There is an interaction. Above all, the children develop quickly, and so does their engagement with the group organism. In the course of their two or three years in the group, they grow in and out of various roles and positions, from observing, attuning, seeking a connection and fitting in, to creating their own space, becoming more independent in relationships, developing the beginnings of a personality and finally letting go of the group. This situation can be compared to a stationary wave which appears under certain conditions in a stream or river, for instance if there is a stone or a tree trunk in the water. The form of the wave remains the same, while the substance of the water flows through it. In a similar way children flow through the form of a group (although, of course, unlike water, children are individuals with their own character and development).

Growing into and growing out of a group in seven steps

Here too the importance of the age of a child is obvious. A baby would not be able to fit into the group, and schoolchildren have outgrown the specific nature of the kindergarten. They become more independent and need different challenges. The relationship of a young child to the kindergarten group goes through several phases of development.

1. In a group where children join at about three and a half years of age, we see the youngest children dream along with everything that happens around them: they *absorb impressions* and *observe* it all. They need a lot of care and security, which is why they enjoy repetition and rhythm so much. It gives them clarity and confidence. In such a situation they are able to integrate spatial images and impressions into their own ether body.
2. The next step is possible when children become more awake to the mutual relationships within the group. They learn to integrate these into their ether body. That allows them to slowly adjust these relationships and *connect* to them by empathising. This adjusting, this attuning may not always be outwardly noticeable. We often have the impression that children do not take part in the classroom, but then we hear that later they act everything out at home, or tell their parents all about it.
3. Children grow toward a third step in their relationship to the group when they begin to notice *individual peculiarities* within the life of the group, such as its habits, and develop their own relationship to these. From there, children can actively create their own place within the life of the group.

THE DEVELOPMENT OF THE CHILD WITHIN THE GROUP ORGANISM

These three steps are related to the process of *growing into* the group. The life of the group is *integrated within the child's ether body* on three levels: perception/thinking, feeling and acting. Of course these qualities are not clearly defined steps in the sequence, but interweave. Nevertheless it is interesting to observe a child and to see where it is in its relation to the kindergarten group. When a child is able to make these three steps it can find its own place within the group. It has become a full member and also brings its own character into the group.

These three levels of integration are necessary for the next step to become possible, because children do not remain forever on this level. They outgrow the group again when they learn to orientate themselves in their surroundings and to arrange/organise it according to their imagination, of course within the limitations of their age. In that process too we can discern three qualitative levels (we skip straight to step 5 here; as we'll see below, step 4 has its own level).

5. When children have found their own place within the group, this position has to be maintained and renewed again and again. It is not like a table that is finished and remains standing without further effort. Children will 'personalise' their place within the group, conserve it, maintain and extend it. They develop their own relationship with toys, bring their own stories to the gnome of ring time, have their own preferences and wishes, their own way of reacting to various situations. Other children know these personal traits and will react to them in particular ways.
6. When children strengthen their own contributions in this way they are ready to make the next step, when they begin to make their relationships with other children more their own. They choose their playmates, form little groups, are able to help younger children find their way into the group, and take on simple tasks for the group.
7. A last level in this process is reached when children begin to form their own conception of themselves and the world. They also wake up to the thoughts of others. They will look at you as the teacher, with slightly different eyes than before: 'Miss Robinson, do you have a husband? A mobile? Did you ever drive through a red light?' Children begin to develop their own imaginations and plans.

That allows them to lead other children in play, and to invent and carry out their own game plans. It is clear that children are now becoming so independent that they are beginning to outgrow the kindergarten. They are ready for school.

So there are also three steps to the process of *growing out* of the kindergarten. These are an expression of increasing independence, of areas in which children can begin to steer their own course: at first they actively stabilise and maintain their own space within the group. Then their relationships with other children are made more personal. And thirdly they become able to implement their own imaginations and plans. These now give a direction to the surroundings, instead of the other way around. That is the moment when they outgrow the kindergarten. The following diagram recaps these steps:

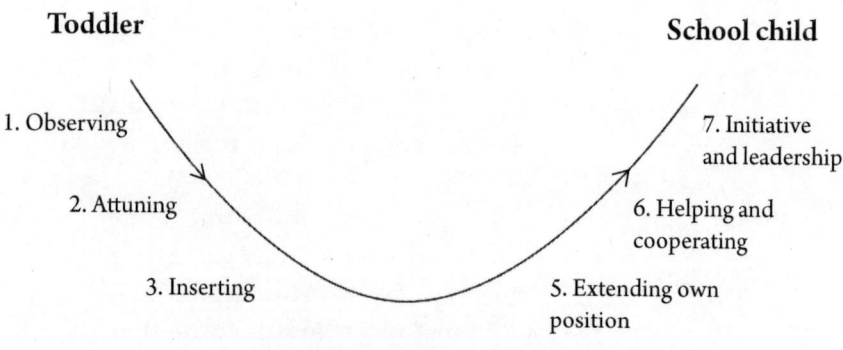

Of course these seven qualities and processes interweave; they do not run along absolutely fixed lines. Looking back at Chapter 8 we can recognise a transformation of the seven life processes in this process of development. Life processes are active in every organism, in the relation to the environment. The life processes working in the human organism as etheric process qualities can also become active in a metamorphosed way as the seven processes of learning.

After the seventh year, children are more capable of independent learning. A teacher can make a conscious appeal to them. However, as we have already seen, the learning path of young children begins with acting and experiencing out of imitation. In the development of the relationship of young children to the group organism, we can recognise the learning processes in a metamorphosed form. We shall once again describe them from this perspective:

— Breathing
    a. This life process deals with the first encounter with the outer world. Air is breathed in, and oxygen is absorbed by the blood in the membranes of the lungs.
    b. The learning process that is the metamorphosis of breathing, facilitates the first perception of and the encounter with the subject matter. Young children absorb the impressions of the outer world through experience. In the relationship to the group, this is the capacity to *observe* and *absorb* impressions of life in the group.

— Warmth processes
    a. Thermo-regulation as a life process attunes inner and outer warmth to each other. This is a deeper interaction with the environment; it does not take place only on the surface. Warmth is also an expression of interest, of an inner engagement.
    b. The metamorphosis of this life process can become active as the capacity to *connect, attune, empathise*. Something can leave us cold, but we can also be 'fired up' by it. In the relationship to the group, young children can open themselves up on this level to the mutual relationships and rhythms of the group and tune in to them, empathise and engage with them. The life of the group penetrates more deeply and comes to life within the ether body of the child.

— Metabolism
    a. On the physical level the task of this life process is breaking down and digesting the substances that are absorbed into the organism from outside.
    b. The metamorphosis of this life process into a learning process is the capacity to *discern, select* and *digest* impressions individually and to process them adequately. Children learn to hold their own, in the face of manifold impressions. In the relationship to the group, this ability

helps young children to be more awake to the peculiarities of the group and to discern its characteristics. A livelier interaction with the group comes about. This is related to the ability to digest the life of the group.

— Secreting

a. This life process is the mysterious capacity of the organism to discern what is its own, and what is alien. This capacity is at work in all the other processes, which is the reason we have not described it as a separate process before. There has to be an organ that perceives what can be absorbed, and what cannot be absorbed and has to be excreted again. The organism opens and closes itself on many levels toward its environment.

b. Metamorphosed into a learning process this becomes the ability in a child to discern and choose whether it wants to connect itself further to a particular subject matter or not. What is important to me? What do I really want to make my own? What choices do I make? Young children also experience this ability to make choices, but on an unconscious level. As they engage more with the group they also acquire an idea of what belongs to the group and what does not. They also develops the ability to make choices within the group as to what is important to it. For younger children, that is of course an unconscious process. The 'I' and the soul still work unconsciously in the vital forces and should not be awoken too soon by questions from grown ups which force a child to make conscious decisions. They will learn this much better later on, if they is allowed to dream a bit longer.

— Maintaining, renewing

a. As a life process, maintaining is the ability to give the organism continuity, to renew the life forces and maintain the balance between all kinds of processes. The individual physical condition is maintained by this life process, and renewed and reinforced time and again.

b. Its metamorphosis as a learning process is the ability to make available and to reinforce something that has been learned. Young children maintain what they have learned by repeating and reliving the experience time and again. In the relationship to the group, this ability is visible in the maintenance and affirmation of their own place within the whole. Some children are a bit quiet, others more voluble; some children are good at telling stories, others can build beautiful structures. Many elements are external and repeated many times, for example, a child's place at table, the picture by the coat peg, its own red sandwich box.

— Growing

a. The life process of growing is much more than just growing in size. In the case of the growth of an organ, it is important that this is attuned to the condition of the other parts of the body, which all grow in their own tempo and direction. There must be an inner image of the growth of this whole and of the place of the organ within this developing organism. It could be described as a social process image on an organic level.

b. The metamorphosis of this is the learning process of extending what has been learned and absorbing the new experiences and insights within the whole. In the relation to the group, this capacity gives young children the possibility to grow inwardly along with their environment and to attune themselves again and again in a more focused way to the others. This happens mainly through the experience of playing with other children: playing with friends, helping, learning to deal with tensions, disappointments, and experiencing joy in playing together.

— Reproducing

a. On a physical level this life process gives the ability to bring forth new life. In a female constitution this expresses itself in a different way than in the male constitution. In young children this process has not fully matured. But the difference between the sexes results in a different foundation of the constitution, which expresses itself in several ways. A group with only girls is different from a group with only boys.

b. The metamorphosis of this life process is a child's ability to use what it has learned in its own way, and create new things with it. In relation to the group, this is the ability of young children to give their own direction to play, to take initiatives in the group, and take the lead using their own concepts. There are often different emphases between in boys and girls.

The diagram on page 154 indicates the relationships between the seven steps. The first and the last steps are polarities, as are the second and the sixth, and the third and fifth. The fourth occupies a middle position, but in a way it is active throughout all the other steps.

The child's own attuning

The question arises how children find their own relationship to each level in a suitable way. In all seven processes, something of the individual nature of the child comes to expression. We can also ask how, on each of these levels, the group receives, absorbs and offers room to the child. The questions at the end of the chapter may help our orientation.

Questions such as these lead us to the unique qualities of a child, which are revealed in these changing areas of development. If we follow a child in this way, certain fundamental gestures can become visible, which remain the same throughout the various phases. Is the child courageous, caring, uncertain, or dexterous? Do they make contact with other children, with nature? What interests and preferences do they have? Gradually we begin to solve the riddle of an individual human being on their way towards their task in life. In childhood the foundation is laid for the abilities this individual will need later on for fulfilling their particular task.

One final set of questions must be addressed, to do with when children are ready to be accepted into the group, and when they have outgrown this particular group-form and are ready for school.

If children are brought into the group too soon, they can be a hindrance. Similarly a connection lasting too long is also an obstacle. The kindergarten must be able to offer room for children at either ends of this spectrum. How do we deal with the youngest children? With new children? With older children in kindergarten? In some countries this question is more pressing, because a wider age-range has to be taken into account.

It is an art in itself to form the organism of a group in such a way that all children can find a place suitable for their development.

THE DEVELOPMENT OF THE CHILD WITHIN THE GROUP ORGANISM

> **Questions for your own research**
>
> **1. How do new children observe the group when they enter it?**
>> How are they perceived by the group and how are they received?
>> How do they open themselves up to their environment?
>
> **2. How do children attune themselves to their environment?**
>> How flexible can the group be to take into account the specific individual nature of a young child?
>> How well do children sense the relations and rhythms of the group and attune themselves to them?
>
> **3. How do children actively become part of the group?**
>> How do they take part, or do they hold back?
>> Which aspects of group life give children the most satisfaction?
>> What do they find more difficult?
>> Which content can they digest and handle actively?
>> Which content do they still find difficult?
>
> **4. What place does a specific child find within the group?**
>> How does the child carry the life of the group?
>> What individual qualities do they contribute?
>> What does the group lack when the child is not there?
>
> **5. How do children form the specific nature of their contribution to the group?**
>> Do they find it easy to create a space for their own character and wishes?
>> What special wishes and preferences do they have?
>> How do these influence the life of the group?
>> What characteristic actions and expressions do they repeat often?
>
> **6. How do children create their own network in relation to other children?**
>> For example, in their choice of friends, groups, their relation to younger children?
>> Do they enjoy playing with other children?
>> How do they deal with disappointments, tensions with others?
>> How do other children treat them?
>
> **7. How do children follow their own imagination and plans?**
>> Is a child able to carry out its own plan or imagination?
>> What imaginings are important to a child?

> Are they able to lead smaller children?
> Do they feel responsible for what happens in the group?
> Are they quite dominant in this?
> What (semi-conscious) images and pictures do they have of themselves and others?

20. The Group Organism Through Time

In the previous chapter we looked at the relationship between the child and the group from the perspective of the child. We can also look at how the organism of the group lives within the child, and at the development the group organism itself. Children that have gone through kindergarten have taken the forms and characteristics of the group into their own ether body. If these are not further maintained, they will slowly diminish in strength or will metamorphose into other forms. That shows the development of the individual human being in relation to its ether body. The group as an etheric organism lives on in that relationship. The being of the group can maintain a certain strength over a longer period of time: it lives on in children that have left the group but the group-form itself is also replenished and fed by new children. It is a constellation of forces, which remains potentially present, even when the children of the group are not physically together.

In this way a child may transcend time and space and suddenly enter the complex of ether forces of the group being. An example of this is when at home, a little girl forgets the immediate surroundings and relives and re-enacts events she experienced in kindergarten. She sings songs, talks with or for other children, re-enacts ring games or a little play. All of a sudden the organism of the class is present.

The independent life of a group organism

It is apparent that a group organism can transcend space and time and work on in a latent way. In certain situations it may surface again, sometimes in unexpected or even vehement ways.

Very interesting in this context is a form of therapy called Family Constellations. In these group sessions someone presents a problem regarding their own family situation. The problem is re-enacted by the person, aided by several other participants, who have no connection with the family in question. The therapist places several volunteers in such a way that they express the relationships within that particular family. That is often sufficient to 'activate' the family organism. The 'actors' feel the tensions and emotions at work in the real family. They begin to feel and speak like the family members, even ones that may have died. Guided dramatic steps may release or break through certain tensions and blocks. This can even have an effect on the actual relations in a family, on people who may not even be present in the therapy session.*

With regard to our present theme this raises several questions: can a group organism potentially work on people who are not a member of the group? And how does the nature of a kindergarten group compare with a family group?

It is also very interesting in the Family Constellations method, that the form, the 'standing wave' of the group organism, can be changed again after it has begun to lead its own life in the sub-conscious. A hardened form acts as a kind of group-double. When the stone is removed, the water can flow more freely, and more natural forms can come about. So we can ask: what causes the group-form, what reinforces the power of the group? We shall return to these questions in the following chapter.

The influence of the group organism on others

The force of a group organism can have an effect on people who are not themselves a member of the group. This was illustrated in a Czech Waldorf kindergarten. The children of the Waldorf kindergarten sometimes spent time together with children from the state school kindergarten, for example when many children were off sick, and it was not viable to have two teachers in the afternoon session for a just few children. One day state school children had to come along on a walk. The Waldorf kindergarten teacher was worried about this mingling because of the totally different cultures of the classes. And at first

---

* The Family Constellations method has led to lively discussions in anthroposophical circles. It is undoubtedly effective. But it is not clear what forces are brought into play and out of which world-view they come. The method does make it very clear that relationships within a group can have enormous power and can lead to personal tensions or blocks. The relationship to such a field of forces is only a limited part of the personality. It does not address the question what the meaning of this relationship might be from the perspective of a person's individual karma. When the release of blocks does not lead to insights into the karmic backgrounds, the same problems may arise again in another form.

there was some restlessness. The teacher decided to do the games her children were used to. This activated the group organism and the other children were too young to take an individual stance against it. It was not long before the children of the state school came and joined in and thoroughly enjoyed themselves. If we offer young children clear forms they can join, they are usually very happy. Similar situations arose at a meal times and during naps. When strong habits are carried through, other children can join in with them.

The group organism in the classroom and in families

What is the particular quality of a kindergarten group compared for example to that of a family? A kindergarten group also has a strong group being, but a child spends only a relatively short time in it. For that reason it will not leave such a deep imprint in the ether body of the child as the group organism of the family. Children only spend a part of every day for a few years in kindergarten. For children, the foundation of life remains the family. They are born into it and they remain there their whole youth.

So the kindergarten group supports the family. It gives the children extra space for development and experience that a family often cannot offer – even more so because many traditional cultural communities are declining, like the church, villages, work communities. If the resulting void is not consciously filled and formed, children may fall prey to consumerist behaviour, stereotypes, or depression and loneliness.

Another difference is that the forms in a kindergarten are consciously filled by a professional educator. The teacher has received specialist training. That may give added support to the carers at home who are untrained and unpaid, but who have to be available always. When there is a good attunement between parents and teachers it can lead to a mutual fructification of the life spheres. And many families these days really need extra support.

The group organism as a social being

As we saw, the effectiveness of the group organism can transcend the actual school hours in the classroom. Once again, many questions arise: does the group organism have its own consciousness? And if so, how does that work on? How can we observe the life of a group organism?

Sometimes the independent existence of the group organism becomes evident in very special moments. The group being of a kindergarten may suddenly assert itself appearing out of a relatively dreamy state, and show its individual initiative.

A kindergarten teacher in Holland once experienced something of this nature when she fell ill and a supply teacher had to be brought in. She was worried the children might mess around without the teacher they were accustomed to. In fact, the opposite happened. The children themselves began to care for the forms and habits of the group, and swept the supply teacher along with them.

Something similar happened to a Slovak kindergarten teacher. She and her colleague usually had clear tasks. Her colleague would do the practical things in the afternoon, such as peeling the fruit for snack time, while she worked with the children. If she asked the children to help, they would refuse. One day her colleague fell ill and she had to do everything herself. She was worried she might not manage everything. At that moment the whole group came to her and out of themselves the children offered to help prepare the fruit.

These changes in the active behaviour of a group occur especially with regard to a useful and intentional reaction of the group to a specific situation. Apparently a reinforced self-consciousness manifests in the group in such extraordinary situations, which is not called upon in ordinary circumstances. So our picture of the being of a group becomes more and more differentiated: it has an inner space, a differentiated inner structure, an effective power, and it can, if needs be, react to its environment in an intentional way. In that reaction it can moreover transcend space and time.

Gaps in time

What would happen if children from a particular group met each other again after five or ten years, for example for a whole week? Of course children from a particular kindergarten group often remain together during their whole time in lower school. In that case the group habits are overlaid by new ones, and the habits from kindergarten time are difficult to recognise. And after thirty years? Would anything of the original tissue of forces still be active? With regard to the mirroring of the life-phases, it is particularly interesting to study how the organism of the kindergarten group works on. Does any aspect of life in the kindergarten resurface in a metamorphosed way in the periods between 35 and 42, and 56 and 63? Those are the years when the first seven year period is often reflected in a person's biography.

In any case the group organism will work on individually in every child. It has made an impression in the constitution of the child that works on during the rest of the child's life. When a child has absorbed through the group organism the habits of making meaningful gestures, being considerate to other children, being able to listen, enjoying beautiful colours and sounds, singing, listening intensely to a story, working in a concentrated way with all kinds of materials, then those are qualities that person will carry for a whole life. That is, of course, true both of group organisms in the classroom, and those of the family.

The mysterious thing about developments in the world of living things is that we cannot really perceive them with our physical senses. They suddenly appear out of an invisible reality. What was founded on a physical level in the first seven years will be, in a metamorphosed form, the basis for the development of the soul in the period between 35 and 42 years. And also for the spiritual development in the period between 56 and 63. Just like in the plant world there is an invisible stream of development, beside the visible stream of development, such as in the transformation from leaf to flower. Where does a rosebud suddenly spring from?

Karmic connections in the group organism

This brings us to yet another level in relation to the group. Anthroposophy acknowledges that human beings go through repeated lives on earth. The experiences in an earthly life are processed in the spiritual world from a moral-spiritual perspective. Rudolf Steiner described a number of connections in this context.

In a kindergarten group too, children meet each others who may have had shared experiences in past lives. Rudolf Steiner indicated that we often meet people from a former incarnation in a different phase of life. On the whole therefore, children in kindergarten may have met each other in a former life as adults. In a kindergarten group certain relationships can come about in which something of this shared past may light up in a transformed way. In a family it is quite likely that there was a previous connection.

Of course we have to be very careful and not draw conclusions too hastily. Our everyday thinking, bound as it is to the physical senses, has no direct access to these insights. Most people have not yet developed the ability to perceive such karmic connections themselves; however that does not mean we cannot use this approach. We can try initially to develop a feeling for connections like these. If we assume the possibility of this reality, we can develop an openness and reverence for the riddles in the relationships between human beings, and empathise with them. This creates a mood of respect for the destiny of every human being. We cannot plan or schedule for such a mood in a curriculum. It is a different, invisible reality in education, working in between the tangible phenomena. In Waldorf education it is very important to understand this.

Preparing, activity, after-care

If we develop a sense for these invisible realities, we can practise dealing with them more and more consciously, such as in the way we prepare an activity, carry it out and digest it afterwards. In this threefoldness of preparation, activity and after-care, sudden leaps of transformation are perceptible too (see Chapter 16). Here too we can come across quite remarkable connections and coincidences, which transcend the physical-causal relationships in time. This is a subject worthy of more extensive exploration. Here I will just mention one example of a kindergarten teacher in Slovakia.

> *This teacher woke up one day with a strong feeling that she wanted to do a certain folk song and a corresponding movement game with the children. That day in her kindergarten, before she could bring it, some children began to sing the song themselves. When she began practising it with them something 'clicked' immediately. After school she talked to a friend who was a teacher in another kindergarten. The friend had just begun the very same song and movement game that day. Some days later she went to church. During the sermon the priest mentioned that particular song, and discussed its background. Pure coincidence?*

This is just one more indication of the mysterious cohesion of the ether world. We mentioned Sheldrake's morphic fields and Jung's synchronicity. In the ether world we are not as separated from each other as we are in the physical world. It is a great task for the future to develop a sensitivity for this and to create space in life for an increasingly conscious handling of this reality.

A kindergarten group as ether organism weaves and works in the ether world, and in that world it is not so sharply separated from its surroundings. It seems that the group can appear in different guises and work meaningfully in various situations. How does a group organism influence a child? What is the healing and nourishing influence of a group on a kindergarten child? How can we care for this organism? These are good questions for further research.

21. The Meaning of the Group for the Young Child

In the previous chapters we saw that a group organism also has a certain *course of life*. This is true for longer time processes, such a the whole school year, and also for the shorter processes within a day, or for each individual activity. There is always an initial time when the group becomes a whole, and there is a moment of winding down, when the energy tails off. There is a time of incubation, a moment of birth and appearance and there is a period of fading, dying and disappearing of the group form. What happens to the group organism, where has it gone?

Time and again there is a rhythmic alternation of appearing and disappearing for outer perception. Nevertheless, something works on in between these moments of appearance. When a ring game is repeated over and over, it becomes stronger. So even between the active moments, something seems to work on.

A biography, the course of a life, always has a certain meaning. For a group too there has to be a reason for its existence, a meaning to its life. When that reason is fulfilled, is lived out, life withdraws again from the group. Groups have two time gestures:

— One is the time gesture connected to the forming of a group or an activity of the group, such as a ring game or a fairy tale. Why is a group begun? Why do we tell a fairy tale? And why that particular fairy tale for those children, at that time? We can talk of the *initiation* of the group organism, or of a certain activity within it.
— The other time gesture occurs every time the group comes together again, when the fairy tale is told. The group organism flows into the form, into the telling of fairy tales. An individual, current time span is connected to this. At what moment is the fairy tale told? For how long can the children pay attention to it? Here we can talk of *activating* of the group organism.

We can compare both gestures in time to the building of an instrument, for example a violin, and the moment we pick up the violin to play it. Let us call them the longer time span and the shorter. For both there is a reason, a cause for their coming about. These two causes are connected, but are nevertheless different. The impulse behind the longer time span (building the violin) is more far-reaching, it is the *raison d'être* of the group, the reason for telling fairy tales in class, the reason for the choice of a certain fairy tale.

The impulse behind the shorter time span (playing the violin) is related to the moment of the day, the particular stream the group is in, at a certain moment. How does the activity fit within the stream? It is interesting to follow how both time spans are connected to each other. In this chapter I want to go further into the function of the longer time span.

There are all kinds of different groups and different reasons for their existence. What is the reason for the existence of a kindergarten group? What can be achieved in such a group that cannot very well be achieved without it?

There is more than one answer to this question of course. One important quality of the kindergarten group as a whole is for example that it forms a sheath in which the child can gain certain experiences. What does this sheath provide?

Support of the ether body

First of all children can have experiences within this sheath that support their ether body. Within the ordered time frame of the group, children can learn to orientate themselves independently with regard to time.

All kinds of habits and rhythms support this ordering of time: they create an independent sphere of life, defining the group as an organism separate from the outer world. We described before how important it is to care for both the inner world of the group, as well as its relationship to the outer world. Some important qualities of the etheric inner world require care and attention.

Strengthening the ether body
Warmth is an important stimulating and nourishing quality in the group. All kinds of things happen all the time, interesting things, joyful things that stimulate activity. The teacher surrounds all these activities with her warm attention. In *The Education of the Child*, Rudolf Steiner

writes that human warmth in education is the force that can help to 'hatch' the organs of young children in the right way.

Another quality that strengthens the ether body is *repetition*. Repetition is a quality very typical for the ether world. Life in a group needs repetition. Repetition creates an organism that is recognisable for those who have become familiar with it. Repetitions also work in *space*: furniture, storage for toys, children's place in the ring, at the table, etc. And of course repetitions in *time*, the daily schedule, the unfolding of activities, and of course the seasons' festivals. Other repetitions can be found in *subject matter* such as the stories, games, the gnome of the class, songs, table grace, etc.

The next aspect that strengthens the forces of the ether body is *rhythm*. That is of course related to repetition, but it is also slightly different. A rhythm comes about when a breathing interaction occurs between different polarities, with a certain direction of development. Breathing is the archetypal rhythm that occurs between concentration (breathing in) and release (breathing out). The activities of a Waldorf kindergarten throughout the day also follow a rhythmic movement, in the alternation between concentration and release, focused inwardly or outwardly, engaging in individual or in communal activities. But there is also a meaningful direction to the whole day.

The forces of the ether body are further supported by a *singular identity*, a concept, an inner direction, an all-embracing idea, in which all activities, pedagogical considerations, treatment of the space, the surroundings, the parents, etc. find an inner cohesion. On the whole the principles of the Waldorf kindergarten give direction to the concept. But people who work with it practically must fill this concept with life. So a particular group of children, with their particular teacher, the particular school and the particular group of parents give a kindergarten group its unique individual character and identity. The more everyone is conscious of this identity, the better it can be given practical substance, and all the different aspects be attuned to each other. If for example we acknowledge the importance of rhythms, then that can be a guide for the interaction with parents and colleagues. If we accept the principle that a kindergarten child should be treated differently from a school child, then we follow that principle in all aspects of the work, not only in the classroom, but also in relation to parents and colleagues. An organism can develop when its identity becomes visible in all the individual parts.

Social development

A second area where the value of a kindergarten group is evident is the social behaviour that can be practised within a group. Children can become acquainted with all kinds of behaviour in the group, such as taking the lead or being led, caring or being cared for, speaking out or listening, considering the whole or keeping their own interests in mind. Within the kindergarten group these roles are still embedded in the etheric organism of the group that offers a space for development in a protecting, harmonising, supportive and stimulating way.

So in a playful way children can learn social skills. In a natural way they learn that there are certain rules and arrangements between people. They can develop a healthy feeling for fairness, for give and take.

Playing, living and acting together are a stimulus for many other areas, such as the development of movement, spatial orientation, inner mobility and imagination.

Individual sense images, images of meaning

A third area is the possibilities for individual identification offered by a group. For example, in play children can compose their own story together with other children, or digest certain experiences. Through the various examples in stories, games and crafts, children receive a rich variety of sense images, with which they can identify through imitation. They make their own choices from this variety, and so develop the conditions for forming a personality, suitable for fulfilling the individual tasks of their lives.

These are three important aspects of a group, and for kindergarten children the ether world forms the basis of this. The kindergarten group derives its sense or purpose from these three areas. Once this has been fulfilled, that particular group form has no more purpose. Children no longer feel the sense, and life ebbs away. Once a game in which a child wants to digest a certain experience has fulfilled its purpose, it no longer feels motivated to do so. So one can ask in relation to the life of a group as a whole and in relation to every single activity: when is it 'finished'? And why? We have to develop a sense of feeling for the inner tension within a process.

Questions for your own research

Questions about the etheric inner life of the group

In which moments did I experience the 'brooding' effects of warmth?
What is my own relationship to warmth? When do I feel warmth?
Where do repetitions occur, in which areas?
Did I consciously introduce them?
Where can more repetition, or less, be beneficial?
When do I feel that a repetition supports, where does it lose its strength?
How do I feel in dealing with repetitions?
Can I really go along with these, or do I switch off? How do I deal with that?
Which rhythms can I observe in working with the children?
What do the rhythms do to the children and to myself?
Are there non-rhythmical moments and activities? What happens in those moments, how are they different?
How do I assess that?
When can I experience a certain identity in the group? How does that express itself?
Is it possible to characterise this identity?
Is the identity active in a wide sense?
Which moments or activities are perhaps not permeated very well with this identity?
What can I do about that?

Questions about the social life of the group

What is the mood like in the group, between the children?
Is there a good and lively attuning and understanding?
Are the children interested in each other?
Is there a lot of quarrelling and restlessness?
Do the children feel accepted by the group, part of the group?
Is there room for their own contributions? How do they do that?
Do they play together a lot?
What roles can I observe generally?
Are they fixed or is there change?
Do I consciously stimulate these changes?
Where and how do I influence the role patterns and why?
What rules are at work within the group?
Where do these rules come from?

What rules do the children follow as if they were natural habits?
Which rules do I perhaps feel uncertain about?
Which rules do the children find more difficult?
Which rules are absent?

Questions about sense images

Which sense images are offered in the group?
Is there a rich variety?
Which sense images do the older kindergarten children absorb?
What kind of sense images are not so available?
How could I try to supply these?
How am I myself connected with the sense images?
With which of these do I feel an affinity, and which do I not relate to?
How do I live into the sense images? What could I improve?

22. Running a Group Together

Until about twenty years ago it was generally the case in Holland that a kindergarten teacher would do the job on her own. She would work with the children from about 8.30 until 12.30. Then there were teacher's meetings, contact with parents, preparation, etc. However, this situation has changed, and there is now more job-sharing where two teachers divide the job between them. In some countries the kindergarten has much longer hours, so there are at least two teachers for each group, one doing the early shift, the other coming in later.

In both situations, teachers will have to adjust to one another, either because they share the job, or because there is a shared presence.

Some thoughts on job-sharing

Job-sharing gives rise to all kinds of questions. The reason for such an arrangement is usually a personal desire of the teacher: they want more free time, to pay less tax, do a course, spend more time with their own children, or whatever. In some cases it became clear that shared jobs did not lessen the load as much as was hoped for. The teachers spend less time in the group, but on the other hand there are a lot of new tasks, because of the hand-over and adjustment. How do they manage that? One teacher used to do a lot of work on her own, now two teachers spend a lot of time attuning and adjusting to each other. They must each have a clear picture of what the other does, and they need to co-ordinate a lot when planning and carrying out the activities. To achieve some continuity in the group, they also have to see the other teacher working with the children. This means a lot of overlap. In some schools the job-sharers arrange to be in the kindergarten together one day a week. The result is that together they work more hours than one teacher on her own.

The needs of the kindergarten group

In a shared job arrangement, the needs of the kindergarten group are adapted to the needs of the teachers. There will have to be compromises. After what we discussed in previous chapters about the ether body of the teacher and of the group, it's obvious that irregularities will have an effect on the ether body of the group organism. A strong group organism has an inner structure full of vitality. This life force is built up through repetition, continuity, rhythm, familiarity, regular habits and an intimate relationship to the teacher. When two people lead a group together, they must accommodate each other as well as they can. This requires attuning on several levels from both teachers.

This may not always be easy. All kinds of unexpected questions may arise in this process of adjusting. A lot will depend on the dedication and openness of the teachers. I do not want to go as far as to advise against this solution. In some cases it is obviously a necessity. If the arrangement works well there can be advantages: it's better to have a healthy, fit team of two than a single, overworked teacher. It is also an advantage in case of sickness, when the familiar partner can step in, rather than a strange supply teacher.

Job-sharing is something that at first sight appears to lead away from the educational ideal. However, it forces us to confront many issues more consciously (something that our times are increasingly demanding). This struggle together may give rise to new ideas and insights that can benefit our working with kindergarten groups. There must be a willingness to tackle these questions, otherwise that can lead to new conflicts. The reason for a job-share was, after all, the wish to work less, or differently, but the job appears to be increasing. A price has to be paid somehow, by the adults or by the children.

Attuning the activities

The teachers will have to attune their activities on several levels. The most obvious are the practical tasks and activities that have to be shared. How do we deal with that? Who does what?

How the days are divided up plays a large part. There are several possibilities. For example: one and four days – two and three – two-and-a-half each – three and three days (with overlap). As the days are divided more equally, the division of tasks becomes less obvious.

One and four days
In a division of one and four, it is clear that the teacher working four days will carry the main responsibility. She will probably do most of the organising tasks, as with a full-time job: colleague meetings, communication with parents, festivals, admin. With the time needed to adjust her work to that of her colleague, it is doubtful whether splitting the job will make her workload much lighter. For a teacher working only one day a week it is difficult to establish a real connection to the group. Her bond with the children, school and parents will probably remain fairly loose. Establishing a rhythm is limited to working a regular day of the week. It is very important to follow at least that one rhythm through, and not change her day of the week.

Two and three days
The division of two and three days is more harmonious, and two-and-a-half days each is of course fully equal. How do they divide the work in this case? For the children regularity, rhythm, peace and clarity, are still important, also in their relationship with the different teachers. That means the teachers' working days should be consecutive, and certainly not alternating. If the teacher's days are fixed, then for the children this means always doing the special weekly-activities with the same teacher. Bread making, painting, etc., are always done on the same day in Waldorf kindergartens. With other activities the teachers will have to alternate. If a fairy tale is told for several weeks, or a certain ring game, then the children will do the fairy tale with the different teachers. It is interesting to see what happens in that case. The teachers' adjusting to each other remains very important.

Three and three days
The solution of three-three is actually the best, especially when the day of overlap is in the middle of the week, Wednesday; then both teachers can observe each other at work and there is a natural transition. The kindergarten in Groningen, the Netherlands, had very positive experiences with this system. An extra dimension enters the cooperation, namely being there at the same time. More about that later.

With a more or less equal division the question of who does the organisational and administrative tasks remains open. More consultation will be needed too, in adjusting the content of the different tasks of the teachers. Often it works out that one of the teachers is mainly responsible.

In some cases it may be a good solution to alternate responsibility, for example in the preparation of the programme of activities. Or there might be a division per activity: for instance, one prepares the fairy tale; the other does the seasonal table. The contact with parents can also be divided between the two teachers.

Shifts

Where there are long days requiring a change of shift (as for instance in the Czech Republic and Slovakia) it has become regular practice in several Waldorf kindergartens to alternate the early and the later shift, and to link it to the allocation of tasks. The teacher on the early shift has the main responsibility for the activities. She prepares the ring game and the fairy tale. The other has the role of assistant and may be in charge of more supportive tasks such as the seasons' table. In an alternating two-weekly rhythm this can work very well. Two times two weeks is about a monthly cycle, a rhythm of the ether body.

In any case, a shared job requires more personal and social flexibility than when working alone. That is one issue the solo teacher does not encounter, and which is often forgotten when beginning a shared job. We often hear the teacher who did not have the main responsibility complain that she wasn't taken seriously, and that she wanted more of a say. On the other hand it can be frustrating for the teacher with the main responsibility, having to involve a colleague more who may not want to do more work, because she is occupied with other things the rest of the week. Arrangements have to be very clear from the beginning.

Two ether bodies, one group

The main Pedagogical Law remains valid when two teachers run a group: the ether body is the main pedagogical tool for working with children up to seven. What does that mean when working together?

We are asleep in our ether body. Our habits are at work there, our basic attitude, our characteristic way of dealing with our environment, our life forces. We touched upon these aspects before. When a teacher works by herself, many of these qualities remain semi-conscious. The teacher can follow her own temperament and her own habits and basic attitude. When two people are involved, two ether bodies are at work in the same 'pond' of the group organism. In that case it is important that the teachers are well attuned to each other. It does not mean that their basic attitude and temperaments must be the same, but there will have to be a certain chemistry between their ether bodies. Indeed, the chemical ether or the musical ether is especially important here. The attuning can be encouraged by agreement on certain habits and ways of working, but that is not all.

Soul and ether body

Things can become difficult when this chemistry is not naturally present. Because we are half asleep in our etheric body, we shall experience a dissonance in chemistry half-consciously too. Something blocks the flow. In my experience people wake up to this when something begins to irritate, to grate. But we wake up on a *soul level*. We begin to connect feelings and images with semi-conscious discomfort, until the moment when we can no longer keep quiet about it. Initially we may say something in an indirect way, or related to a limited aspect of the problem: 'You know, you should set more of a boundary for the children,' 'You do seem to be rather gloomy a lot of the time,' 'It doesn't always have to be so exact, does it?' 'I'd appreciate it if you did not leave the classroom in such a mess,' 'Could we keep the cups in another place?'

The situation may develop in different ways. If we remain on the level of irritation, the situation may worsen, the tensions can escalate. Blocks and distrust may grow. These will have an effect on the ether sphere in which the children have to be carried. A good alignment is not only pleasant on a personal level, it is also a precondition for working well on a professional level. If there is mutual openness and honesty, good conversations may lead to more understanding and better alignment. This communication is necessary, but still takes place on a conscious soul level. Pitfalls and illusions can dog this kind of communication. Many books have been written about this subject. How can we find our way from there, back to the ether body?

Simultaneous presence

If both teachers are present in the group at the same time, this problem may arise in a different way. If they meet each other in the group itself, then the working of both ether bodies can be experienced in a more direct way:

> A Slovak kindergarten teacher had to bridge a period where she had no classroom for her group, and could only take on a few children. She found temporary accommodation in a private home. From a financial point of view it was not possible to run such a small group together with a colleague. So she had to manage on her own, from seven in the morning till three in the afternoon. During this time she formed an intimate bond with the children and was able to create and maintain all activities. She could follow her own feeling for time and her sense for the group organism.
>
> After a while more children joined and they could afford to employ a second teacher. The new teacher had less experience and a different fundamental attitude in her ether body. She gave less form, provided fewer boundaries and was connected to the group far more loosely. For the first teacher this situation was far more exhausting than working by herself, even though the actual workload was less. Inwardly she had to divide her attention time and again. This kept waking her up on a soul level, distracting her from her etheric connection with the group.

Sharing the job of the teacher does not always have a positive effect on either children or teachers. Nevertheless there are instances where it works very well. It demands greater clarity and effort in adjusting and aligning, and a willingness to really know each other. A Czech kindergarten teacher described it.

> I am so grateful to be working with Anna now. For years I had problems, and I even had the group on my own for a year. Now with Anna it works very well. She has more pedagogical knowledge, I have more practical experience. We complement each other very well. If she is teaching and I come into the classroom I feel: yes, this is right, this is how it should be. We have very good and clear agreements on how we work. It often happens that one of us comes to school with a certain idea, and that the other has already prepared it, without either of us knowing. Once we even came to school with the same new blouse.

In this case the alignment of inner attitudes creates a communal organism, which works on from the subconscious (or super-conscious?). But that does not happen by itself. There are many details we can arrange and align together. This begins even before the children have come in. A kindergarten teacher from Holland relates.

> *My day begins well before the children come into the classroom. With my assistant we prepare the space and all the necessary practicalities. We also say a verse as preparation for the day. In this way we attune ourselves inwardly to our work with the children.*

Because the ether body is the pedagogical tool for teaching young children, consciously or unconsciously, it means we have to have a professional attitude to it. It is part of our profession to learn to look at it objectively. Shared jobs and cooperation demand a professional basis of trust which allow such questions to be discussed openly. That is a great challenge for the future! How do we deal with such conversations? How can we manage them professionally and hold back prejudices that may be too personal? How can we form a clear judgment that can become the basis for alignment with the other? In the next chapter we shall discuss this further.

23. Forming Judgments when Working Together

If things do not flow naturally with a colleague in a shared job, it is necessary to have a closer look at cooperation. To prevent getting caught in all kinds of soul struggles, we can try following certain guidelines in these conversations. The main purpose is gaining a professional insight into the ether body of the two teachers. Several books and articles have been written on how to form good judgments. One way can be to divide the conversation in four steps. It may seem a bit cumbersome, but in the long run it saves time and energy:

— *Observing:* Over a period of time both teachers gather observations which they think have to do with the functioning of the ether body.
— *Creating an image:* The second step is integrating the separate observations into a coherent image (see for example the tree image exercise, below).
— *Forming a judgment:* Now they can try to bring this image into inner movement, for example by asking it all sorts of questions. How does this image work in different situations? What do they make of it from a professional perspective? In what respects is this image healing, nourishing, inspiring, supportive, and where do tensions arise?
— *Conclusions and decisions:* What does this mean in practical terms for their work? What can they improve, what agreements can they come to? What learning goals can both teachers set themselves on the basis of these conclusions, this judgment?

These questions can acquire an extra dimension when two teachers share a job. They could, for example, both follow this process individually and then repeat it from the perspective of the mutual alignment as a basis for working with the children:

— 1. *Observing:* What do we observe in the moments of alignment?
— 2. *Creating an image:* What image of the alignment do these separate observations offer?
— 3. *Forming a judgment:* What feeling does this image give us? Where does it work in a positive, stimulating way, where do tension and friction arise?
— 4. *Conclusions and resolutions:* What does this mean for our working together? What can we improve, and how?

Questions with regard to observation

It is not a bad thing to allow observations to arise spontaneously. Then issues will probably come to the surface that evoke a direct feeling. We can also guide our observations with the help of certain questions. The questions are like little lamps making aspects of the 'alignment space' visible. The examples of questions at the end of the chapter may be helpful. We can of course ask other questions too, addressing different aspects of our working together.

Questions with regard to forming an image

Here we synthesise all the separate observations into one image. We look, for example, at whether there are certain recurring themes in all observations, or a certain fundamental attitude. It can help to look from the perspective of the polarities of the types of ether and the elements, as listed in the questions at the end of the chapter.

We can probably find more polarities and combinations. It is also valuable to try and find a cohesive personal attitude in these qualities, a fundamental mood, and a style. These are not real *judgments*, but are attempts to form a truthful inner picture. In a fully-fledged organism, all qualities contribute. We can also ask which qualities emphasise the alignment, which qualities get less attention and which point to tensions and differences.

Another way to bring to life the process by which we form an image of the alignment between teachers, is the tree image exercise (below).

Questions in relation to forming judgments

In the third step we do try to form judgments. We try to 'dramatise' the images we have created, to bring them into inner movement. Feeling plays an important part in this.

> — What do I feel when contemplating the image? It is not only a question of what I feel myself (this is not therapy), but more the feeling as the sensor for a *professional ideal* and in particular with regard to the area of the ether body.
> — What aspects give me a good feeling, where are there tensions? Can I characterise both?

That means both the teachers need to have some clarity about their professional ideals, because the judgment will be related to that. Teachers do not have to be the same. There are teachers with a melancholy temperament, or a phlegmatic or sanguine temperament. Everyone has their own fundamental personal attitude and constitution, and that is as it should be. The question here is to what extent this constitution can serve the educational process. A lot has been said and written about the pedagogical principles of the Waldorf kindergarten approach. We may assume that teachers have formed some idea of this in their training. If not, they won't be able to form good professional judgment, and will have to defer to the judgment of their better-equipped colleague.

To form a judgment we compare the image we created out of our observations to the educational ideal. A conversation along those lines requires a basis of trust and a positive attitude towards our colleague, and towards our own limitations. After all, no one is perfect. We must be willing to strive for insight into human nature, and to work on ourselves as a professional. That is the foundation of Waldorf pedagogy. If we do not have that attitude, that willingness, it may be better not to work in a Waldorf school.

If there are two teachers, there is the advantage that they can help each other, by asking each other questions. These questions can help form their own judgments. The one asking the questions can practise taking the other's point of view, and by asking questions help her colleague come to her own conclusions. That is a good exercise for developing a sensitivity that can also be useful when observing children.

So it is not a matter of judging the other. But we can express our feelings and opinions of the work of the other, and the mutual alignment of our work. What the other person does with our feedback is up to them. If this were not the case, individual freedom would be encroached upon. When someone is given the space to take a step out of their own free will, both colleagues can be pleased. If the step is forced, in whatever way, it is not a cause for celebration. The 'I' was not given a chance.

Questions with regard to conclusions and resolutions

Here too we can differentiate between conclusions and resolutions with regard to our own work, and the ones we arrived at together about the alignment between the work of each.

To begin with it is important to be clear about responsibilities. The one who is responsible for certain tasks will make the decisions relating them. Of course they work best if the opinions of their colleague are taken into account. With regard to our own work, we can only draw our own conclusions and, for example, decide to change something.

If there is a great discrepancy between the fundamental attitudes of both colleagues, for instance if one is very strict and the other quite casual, then we have to come to some agreements, for example, about the boundaries we set the children in various situations, about certain rules, etc.

But the ether body is not a machine that can simply be adjusted. It takes time and will-power to change something in this realm. It is a very modern task, this waking each other up, to learn from each other, and to learn to deal with differences, to accept the other person as they are and also acknowledge and integrate our own limitations. So there is a tension between the ideal we try to attain time and again, and the understanding and compassion for the imperfections in each of us.

From a professional perspective there have to be certain limits as to what is acceptable. Tensions may arise between colleagues that can be treated as a path for development to a certain extent. In the pedagogical relationship with young children, these tensions are disturbing and can hinder or prevent a naturally flowing ether sphere. If cooperation between two colleagues really does not work, another solution must be found. When conversations reach a deadlock in that respect, it may be better to ask for help from outside to find a solution.

The tree image exercise

One aid when forming judgments as discussed above, is the following exercise. Once we have made a number of separate observations of the working of one another's ether body and the alignment between them, we can try painting them as cohesive images, for example first an image of the two ether bodies and then an image of the alignment between them. Such images can provide another way to come to a conversation, and perhaps to avoid soul conflicts that could otherwise arise. These images can be painted from the perspective of their colour moods. If that is difficult, we can try to paint a tree for each ether body separately, and then discuss these images.

A tree is, in a certain way, an etheric image, connecting heaven and earth: the trunk is the most hardened part of the tree, but in this hard trunk the sap flows, maintaining life. The trunk and the branches are the expression of that flowing-image, which is most noticeable in winter. In the shape of their lines we can observe the flow from below upwards, from centre to periphery.

On the other hand there is the crown, with a more enveloping, spherical form. This indicates the peripheral space in which the branches move from out of the earth. That side, that image of the tree is more apparent in summer. In it, the relationship with the cosmos becomes visible, working from above downward, from outside inwards.

What kind of a conversation is there between these two? That tells us a lot about the tree. Are the branches influenced deeply by the crown? Are they straight, or twisty? Do they become very fine towards the end, like the branches of the beech? Is the crown round or is it more elongated? Is it transparent to light, air and life? Or is it more closed off and solid? In this way all kinds of qualities, emphases and relationships may be expressed in the image of the tree as an organism.

A next step could be to paint or draw the two trees close to each other. They will have to share and fill the same space. How would they grow in and through each other? Do they take away the light from each other, or deny each other food from the soil? If we look around in nature we can come across beautiful trees growing right next to each other, forming a fully integrated crown, out of two separate trunks. Sometimes there are different layers of growth: a high tree with a little bush underneath. How do they enter into a 'conversation'? What kind of an environment do they create? Sometimes even the trunks are intertwined.

What is the ideal alignment between teachers in a kindergarten group? When both colleagues paint an image of their alignment and discuss it, they can try to paint and image of the ideal alignment between these trees.

They can then each paint how their trees could grow toward that ideal: where should there be more vitality? Where more form and regularity? Or more connection to the earth? Where a more compliant alignment? Where does it need pruning or cutting back?

Questions for your own research

Observation from the perspective of imitation

Do the children imitate the teachers in different ways? (for example in mood or gestures?)
Do the teachers give different examples? How do these examples differ?
Do the children imitate differently when there is one teacher, than when they are both present?
Do the children imitate one teacher more than the other?
How does that work on the group as a whole?
Which teacher leaves a stronger mark on the whole group?
Does that differ according to the activity?

Observation from the perspective of the relation to the space

What aspects of the classroom does each teacher take care of?
How does she do this? (Carefully, casually, precise, consciously?)
How are these aspects attuned to each other? Does a whole come about in the end?
Which teacher changes the classroom more often? Do you have an agreement about that, conscious or unconscious?
What effect do the activities of my colleague in the classroom have on my ether body? How is that for my colleague?
How does each teacher feel when they are alone in the classroom? How when they are there together?
Do we each have a particular place in the classroom when we are there together, or alone?
What do these places look like? Where are they in the classroom?
How do the children move with regard to these places?

> **Observations from the perspective of the four elements and four ethers**
>
> How is the alignment between the teachers with regard to warmth, engagement, dedication, penetrating the whole, the vitality? Which ideals fire you up?
>
> How does the alignment function with regard to the forms, the practical concepts, the ideas about the design and organisation of the classroom and the programme (light ether)?
>
> How flexible are the teachers with more or less fixed boundaries (air)?
>
> How does the alignment work in the area of rhythms, imagination, play, processes, of encounters in the process, in the moment? How do we interact with one another? (music ether)
>
> How does the alignment work in the area of the flow, regularity, the cohesion and habits (water)?
>
> How does the alignment work in the area of purpose, of educational principles, the connection to spiritual reality, moral force, an eye for the essential, the inner meaning of activities (life ether)?
>
> How does the alignment work in the area of practical realisation, dealing with materials (earth element)?

24. Life Forces and Job-sharing

Split attention

Modern life, with all its stress, difficult issues and fast impressions has a tendency to tear human beings apart, to shatter them. In Chapter 22 we mentioned the kindergarten teacher in Slovakia who experienced a strongly split attention when a new teacher joined the group. This split is an important issue when working together with another adult in the kindergarten group. A Dutch kindergarten teacher relates:

> *I always arrive in the classroom half an hour early. This allows me to go through the whole space and connect to everything. I water the plants, adjust all kinds of objects, look at materials or hang up a decoration. This really allows me to arrive in the space and in myself. I can always feel when other people have been in the classroom. Then it feels as if there are holes in my relationship to the space and objects. Then I always feel the need to penetrate and fill everything with my own attention.*

How can we achieve such an intense connection if we share a group with a colleague? How do we overcome the split, and how do both colleagues achieve an undivided presence and attention? What do we need to achieve this? It is an interesting area for further research. The qualities of the ether body we discussed in previous chapters will show the way, such as warm engagement, regularity, repetition, rhythm, and clear ideas.

This splitting of the attention is a real issue in modern life. The 'zap' culture makes people flightier and their attention span shorter. Really peaceful moments are increasingly rare, when we can be fully present in what we are doing. A lot of thoughts swirl through our heads, about work, family, the media and the many things we feel we have to keep up with. We demand ever more from life: more choice in foods, going out, hobbies, clothes, materials and gadgets for the house, transport, communication, etc. We reach a certain limit in what we can absorb and integrate, although this varies from person to person. This limit wakes us up and calls on us to make conscious decisions on where we focus our attention. Here too we are asked to make conscious decisions. If we don't, we threaten to drown in all the impressions, and lose touch with ourselves. In this sense we can be grateful to our hectic modern life, for it gives us a chance to develop.

Coherence and health

The attention, and the intensity of our presence have a lot to do with our relationship to our own etheric body. If we set ourselves clear, delineated boundaries in our life, we can be much more present with our full attention. The flighty soul on the other hand exhausts the etheric forces, and leaves it ragged and filled with holes, through which alien influences may penetrate, such as viruses. Our health is also connected to the etheric body. Because children up to seven have not yet built up an independent ether body, and are dependent on ether forces in their environment, the quality of our relation to them has a direct effect on the ether bodies of both the children and the educator. Working with children over seven is different. Often there is not enough understanding and consciousness for this special aspect among educators and politicians.

Forty years ago the sociologist Aaron Antonovski did research into the origins of health, and introduced the concept of *salutogenesis* (from the Greek *salus*, health, and *genesis*, origin). According to Antonovski, health is strongly related to what he calls a 'sense of coherence', the feeling of cohesion. On a biological level it is our ether body that creates cohesion and balance in all the processes and functions of the organism, time and again. An enormous wisdom and power of coordination is required for this. But this all happens outside our consciousness. On the other hand, this capacity is increasingly under pressure from the 'zap' culture we mentioned. That is why our health is becoming more and more dependent on conscious choices. When working with a group of young children this is a very acute issue too. The more we manage to create cohesion on all kinds of levels, the more we give scope to the ether forces.

With that in mind it is interesting to ask, what makes the teacher's job more stressful, what makes them tired? What gives them energy? We received the following answers to these questions.

I get tired:
- when my ideas of what I want to happen are too fixed, and the children want something different. For example: a little boy wanted to play 'drums' all the time. Finally I gave in, letting him play in a corner where he did not disturb other children. (Sometimes letting go is important, but also allowing something to happen and setting boundaries. Then we integrate it within a space created by our 'I'.)
- when dealing with a director, trustees or authorities who keep demanding things I do not want, such as working with someone I do not get on with, or if I am not allowed to light a candle in the classroom, or to use wool, or children are not allowed to play with a hammer and saw, or I am not allowed to serve food in my classroom, or children from another class are simply dropped into my group.
- of all the form filling and paperwork.
- of a colleague working from a different background.
- of difficulties and tensions with a colleague in a shared job.
- of parents coming into the classroom.
- when I cannot explain to parents what their child needs.

I get energy:
- when I receive a compliment.
- from working with the children themselves.
- when I have made a work plan and it is successful.
- when I feel heard and understood.
- when there is the right chemistry with my job-sharing partner.
- when our team functions well and everyone respects the others.
- when colleagues or parents agree on ideals or follow the same ideal.

In all these examples, the sense of coherence plays a part, the feeling of coherence on different levels. Coherence with our own ether body: our habits, our ways of working, our attitude to life, and our fundamental mood. Coherence with our colleagues, with parents, the organisation, society, our own insights and ideals. When cohesion is somehow missing, we have to make a conscious effort to re-create it. If we fail, one of our colleagues will languish, or the organism will fall apart: the initiative has no chance of survival and looks for another organisation, the job-sharing colleagues separate, a parent takes their child from the school.

It is interesting to note that the idea of job-sharing comes from a wish for a lighter load, when it all seems too much. But often this solution brings just what one hoped to avoid! There is more dissociation, more tasks and possibly more tension. It takes a certain amount of commitment, continuity and engagement to overcome all this.

And the children?

As we mentioned in Chapter 22, the idea of a job-share did not arise from an educational insight or the children's need, but out of a need of the adults. Of course this arrangement has repercussions on the quality of the work with the children.

> A Dutch teacher told about a conflict she had with her job-sharing colleague. It had dragged on for a long time without being discussed, until at length they talked about it. The children had mirrored the tension. They had lots of conflicts and there wasn't a very good atmosphere. They imitated the conflict in their play, although the teachers, who alternated, did not quarrel in front of the children. When the teachers managed to improve their working together, the children became more positive too.

What does a situation like that do to the children? Of course it is ideal when everything runs smoothly and harmoniously, when there is clarity and a good alignment. After all, the children experience inwardly what the adults carry in themselves. On the other hand, if we manage to talk honestly and openly about our differences, and to find an alignment which can function right through into the etheric sphere, the children will have experienced something very essential. They learn it is possible as human beings to come to a new understanding and a new alignment when there are tensions, or differences in the 'I'-forces. This gives them the trust they all need so badly, that after a problem all can be well again.

Being approachable and committed

Working with young children, there is a danger that the alignment between the two teachers takes so much time and attention, it cannot sink back into the deeper layer of the ether body. After all it can be very interesting to talk about feelings. But in the context of the work with young children, it is only useful when it helps the ether sphere to flow again. After all the real task is to strengthen the ether sphere: our own ether sphere, and in relation to our colleagues, the parents, the organisation, society.

If we manage that, we will have created a firm basis from which to deal with our responsibilities. This is especially important for the children. Young children need the security of feeling that their carer is approachable, not only outwardly, but also inwardly. They need this to be able to 'arrive' in their own ether body. Children living in a zapped up environment will have difficulty building up a strong and well-formed ether body. They will be disabled, not physically, but etherically. With such a weak, shaky and immature foundation they may have constitutional problems for the rest of their lives. This confronts adults with the question, what is really most important thing in life?

Children need their parents to be approachable, and they need their teacher to be approachable too. This means being fully present, carrying the world of our class and of the child with us and within us. This presence does not stop after school. It does not mean we can't do anything else the rest of the day, other than think about our children. It has more to do with the quality of the connection. Somehow, somewhere the children are always around. We take them with us into the night and meet them there too. If we live consciously with this fact, miracles can happen, also in our own development.

This approachability has obviously become a problem for more and more people. They look for variety, entertainment, diversion, and shorter working hours so they can manage. 'De-stressing' has become a catchword, understandably so. But whether that really helps feelings of unease, tiredness and dissatisfaction is rather doubtful. Perhaps working less can relieve stress up to a point. The inner fulfilment we attain when we are wholly approachable leads to different quality of presence. It makes us stronger. In spite of all the fragmentation, people are beginning to feel the need for reality, authenticity, for true meaning. If we enter into a real, committed relationship with a child or a group of children, it may limit us. There are only so many hours in a day. But this deep investment does give us a greater chance of a true encounter, with ourselves, with the children and with others. It is a theme of our time to develop consciousness in that realm. If we manage to find a new relation to our ether body, we may also be able to help develop healthier forms of community and society. Working with young children especially can become a daily path of initiation towards a new culture.

Part V

Reflections

25. Waldorf School Children are Healthier

Recent health research showed that children brought up according to anthroposophical principles, living in an anthroposophical environment, and going to a Waldorf school are usually healthier than other children. They suffer less from infectious diseases or allergies. What are the reasons for this?

In the past forty years, the incidence of allergies, eczema and asthma has risen significantly. Children especially battle with inexplicable infections, viruses and allergies. Science has been studying this for a long time, but so far found no clear explanations.

One team of researchers studied differences in health in relation to the environment where children were brought up.[*] A total of 6630 children were studied in five European countries (Germany, Sweden, Netherlands, Switzerland and Austria). Two-thirds of these children lived in an anthroposophical cultural environment; one third of all children lived in the countryside. The parents had to complete extensive questionnaires, collect samples of dust from the floor and from beds, and several blood tests were performed on the children.

The research showed that children of families with an anthroposophical life style suffered 20 to 30 percent less from hay fever compared to other schoolchildren. For allergies, the difference was 32 compared to 39 percent. For asthma the research showed no significant difference.

Of course we have to ask what causes these differences, as the answer could indicate causes as well as possible treatment for these diseases. Further research was done into the lifestyle of the families. Some marked differences became clear:

For example: 40 percent of Waldorf children had never used antibiotics, compared to only 15 percent of other children. For allopathic anti-inflammatory drugs, such as paracetamol (acetaminophen), the

---

[*] D. Schram-Bijkerk, *Microbial agents, allergens and atopic diseases*, Institute for Risk Assessment Sciences, Utrecht University 2006.

difference was 43 percent compared to 8 percent. One quarter of all Waldorf children had been vaccinated against childhood diseases, such as measles, mumps, and rubella, compared to three quarters of other children. A third of Waldorf children did indeed get measles, compared to a tenth of other children. The differences were most obvious in Germany, Netherlands and Sweden. In Austria the differences were less significant.

In diet, too, there were differences: three quarter of Waldorf children regularly ate organic food, compared to only one quarter of other children.

Tentative confirmation

The scientists carrying out this research consider the results as a tentative confirmation of the validity of the anthroposophical approach. This maintains that allowing children to go through infectious diseases helps them build up a strong immune system. That is the reason their parents give them fewer antibiotics or antipyretics. In a sterile environment, children cannot build up their immune system properly. This view is reinforced by the fact that children growing up in the countryside build up a stronger immune system than children in towns, although (or because of?) the fact that they come into contact with more bacteria. Vaccinations prevent children from getting to grips with normal childhood diseases, and strengthening themselves in the process. Organic (or biodynamic) food also supports children's own life-forces. This must of course not be taken as an encouragement to simply ignore basic hygiene.

Apart from these physically demonstrable differences there are other, less tangible differences in lifestyle, which also have an effect. Babies especially need rest, regularity, rhythm and a healthy diet. Chemical additives in food cause unrest and aggression. One very controversial additive for example is Aspartame, which is used as a sugar substitute in many products advertised as healthy (for example soft drinks, yoghurt, ice tea, chewing gum and other sweets).

The flood of impressions children receive from the media is destructive for the healthy development of the immune system. This is not only because they invite aggression, or provide children with other undesirable examples of behaviour, but also because children cannot develop an inner connection to these lifeless images. It is not only the content, but also the actual looking at a screen that has a negative influence on the constitution and the formation of the brain, especially in children. These impressions cannot be digested properly through children's own activity such as movement and play, so they fester on in their constitutions. They will express themselves later in the form of allergies, aggression or hyperactivity.

Parents as carriers of culture

As this research shows, a new culture has to begin with the parents. The small conscious decisions made in a family setting, create a culture. It is not a matter of proclaiming dogmas and, for instance, banning all media. Depending on children's age, different pedagogical attitudes are needed. But an insight into the effects of food, medicine and the media on our children and ourselves is very important. Do we as parents and teachers have weaknesses and addictions? On the basis of these insights everyone can decide for themselves what they can and are prepared to justify.

26. The Pivotal Point

In this study we've looked at the ether body from different perspectives, related to pedagogical meaning. In everyday life we don't have to change our ether body. We all have very different constitutions, and that is fine. It is our individual choice to work on our ether body. But if our ether body is a professional tool or instrument, working with young children for instance, things are different. Then we have to look at it from a professional perspective and judge it from that perspective too. We will often encounter situations that demand something different than what we want or feel like. Then it is important to act out of what the situation demands, and to hold back our own wishes. The etheric body becomes subservient to the demands of the situation.

For instance, we feel like a ring game with some nice movement, but we sense that the children would cross a boundary and lose themselves, and we have to hold back and remain centred so that the children can remain centred too. Or we are tired and would like to hold back a little, but the children are lively and cheerful, demanding lively attention and engagement. How do we deal with that?

The pivotal point

In our workshops we do movement exercises that allow us to consciously live through and process these moments. What happens when the leader wants to do something different from what the group wants? Initially we may try to communicate, for instance, our own rhythm onto the group in different ways. If we do not succeed, we may get irritated, or we despair. That is a feeling we get when we think that the group has to do what is nice and good for us. If that does not work we must accept it and give up our approach. This may at first be painful. But the group has its own power, its own force, and it is not always easy or desirable for a teacher to change this. We have also noticed that if we manage to let go of our own wishes (whether we are forced to or choose to) a whole other world can open up. If that happens, things can become unexpectedly pleasant and relaxing. We may, for example, be surprised to find that a different tempo is pleasant too, and we begin to open up more to the whole. It may also liberate us from our own one-sidedness and have a refreshing, revitalising effect. This moment of letting go of our own wishes is what I call the *pivotal point*.

There were several teachers in our workshops and courses who, through this focusing on the ether sphere, came to a different attitude in their work with children.

> *One kindergarten teacher had a boisterous class with 17 older children, lots of little self-conscious 'me's. During the course she found a deeper, peaceful layer of the ether sphere. It made her feel the class had to be lulled back to sleep a little. This meant she had to hold back a little, because by nature she herself liked variety and liveliness. So she practised the new orientation with the children. She did more ring games, but holding back more, and with lots of repetition. It worked, and the children too found rest in this deeper sphere of life. When she had made this inner change, she found to her own surprise that she herself actually enjoyed it more.*

The pivotal point in the kindergarten group

Not only the teacher, but also the children can experience such pivotal points. But they cannot yet deal with them in a conscious, independent way. That is the case with children individually, but also the kindergarten group as a whole. It is fascinating to experience that a group of children as a whole can make an inner switch that is meaningful in a particular situation.

> *A kindergarten teacher in Holland introduced a ring game, which we had practised in one of our courses. Some of the boys said: 'that's silly' and did not want to join in at first. The teacher persevered and gradually a serene atmosphere descended that was good for the children too. Even the boisterous boys began to join in enthusiastically. After a while one of them said to the teacher: 'Cool, isn't it?'*

It is interesting why this mood appeared during this particular game. It might be because this particular game had a dreamy and refined mood but with a good balance. Another reason may be that the teacher herself had changed and had found a different approach.

The pivotal point may occur in quite a different way too. A Czech kindergarten teacher related following.

> *When I try to remember a special ring time, I think of the following situation. We were doing a ring game with the children, when the circle broke. I was leading them in quite a difficult spiral. So at that moment I was stuck in the middle. A girl of four broke free and grabbed the tail of the group and all of a sudden she took the lead. She pulled the whole group along into the space at quite a speed. Because I was stuck I could not do anything. I had to make an inner switch and let go, let myself be drawn along. I had become the tail! Just when the group threatened to fall apart, I was able to catch the girl, and we formed a circle again, in which the game calmed down. We were overjoyed because there was a moment of uncertainty and unexpected initiative. That made it exciting. But it was satisfying too that we could end the game as a circle. For me this meant that I had to twice make a switch in my relation to the group.*

Because she made an inner switch twice, went along with the group, and also took the lead again at the right moment, an intense movement organism came about. This would not have happened had she broken off the game. Another Czech kindergarten teacher told the following.

> *Sometimes it drives me to despair when things do not go the way I want. I had a moment like that when we had to clear up after free play, and it was actually quite late. It was very chaotic and the children refused to help. I did not know what to do. At that moment something in me changed. I let go of my stress, of the feeling that I could not save the situation. I just took the toys nearest to me and began clearing up by myself. All of a sudden the mood in the class changed. The children became calmer and they began helping with great dedication. In no time everything was cleared away and in its place.*

So, living through the pivotal point means firstly, letting go of the old images, expectations and feelings; secondly, waking up and being able to live in the new situation that wants to come about; and thirdly to re-connect with the demands of the situation. The more consciously we can do that, the more effective and beneficial it becomes.

Children and pivotal points

Children cannot always handle these situations and need help. They are dependent on those around them and usually they do not make the decisions. That means they experience several pivotal points every day, such as when their play is interrupted because the clock indicates it is time to stop. Or when they have to come to the shops because they cannot stay at home alone. There are countless examples where children are forced to give in to the demands of adults. We must remember that children cannot create new connections from a clear consciousness, the way adults can. But they do have to adjust to new situations time and again. It is right of course that adults make the decisions. But are the needs of children always taken into account? It is tempting to follow our own urges if we are in charge and make the decisions. This responsibility means that we must be able to deal with our own pivotal points. In other words: we must be able to weigh up our own needs against the needs of the children, and strike a balance. If children lose out too much in this balance, it means they carry a greater burden. Children need understanding and protecting against the speed of modern life with its impressions, temptations and wishes. If they are to learn to deal with pivotal points later in life, they must be given the space to learn to trust their own judgment and feeling. When that is constantly overwhelmed, they will find it difficult to become independent later.

This does not mean we must always give in to children. Sometimes a clear decision and instruction can help them surmount an inner blockage. Here is an example from a mother.

> We were picking up my daughter who had been staying at granny's. She did not want to come home, she wanted to stay longer. But she really couldn't. She became impossible, totally stuck in her wish and her anger. In the car on the way home she burst into tears. She cried a long time until all of a sudden she became quiet. Her mood changed instantly. All of a sudden she was incredibly positive, open and helpful, and longed to go home.

The girl felt that the decision to go home was right and she was grateful that her mother gave her the security of a right and just decision. Sometimes children must be helped out of their obsessive state. There are different reasons why children get stuck in an attitude like that. Two important factors are:

1. Young children are driven largely by their own organism, their vital forces. These can be quite compelling. Children in this state are not malicious, they are really asking for help. If they get cramps or suddenly need the toilet, you can't pretend the feeling isn't there.
2. Because the higher parts of the children's constitution have not been born yet, children are very dependent on their environment, which they imitate extensively. Children's motives lie to a large extent outside themselves. Young children can be helped by distracting their attention, or changing their environment and bringing them into another space. It is also important to check if there is anything around that stresses and disturbs them.

An obsessive state can be very powerful. How can we help children free themselves from it? In his Curative Education course, Rudolf Steiner describes how this may be done. An upset and over-excited child can be taken by the arms and held still for a time. A moment will come when the child stops struggling and the state is 'turned', a pivotal point. The child may cry but it will be grateful to come back to itself. A kindergarten teacher in Holland discovered this out of her own intuition:

> *I had a very noisy boy in my group, who sometimes drove me to despair. When he threatened to get overexcited, I took hold of him, held him firmly against me and did not let go. After a while something would turn in him and he began to breathe more calmly. He may not have liked it at first, but I did get the impression it was good for him and that he was grateful for it.*

In such cases it would be interesting to find out what a child's family situation is. Do the parents set the child enough boundaries? What kind of physical contact is there in the family? For example if a parent address children in an intellectual way too soon, they may lack inner peace and stability which they actually long for on a physical level. In the first years after birth the bond with the parents is very important in this respect. If there is a gap in this realm, then the relationship to their own physicality remains unsure. The resulting disquiet may later hinder children's concentration and openness to their surroundings.

Questions for your own research

Can I recognise any of my own pivotal points from past experience?
Are there certain recurring themes or experiences in these points?
How did I deal with them? Do I find it easy to let go?
What did I experience when it worked?

The pivotal point in the group

Have I ever experienced pivotal points in my group?
Can I describe them very accurately?
In what kind of moments did they happen?
Is there a similarity between these moments?
How was I connected to these moments in my role as teacher?
What effects did it have on the group?

The pivotal point and the children

Did I ever notice the children going through pivotal points?
At what moments did they occur, were there certain themes to these moments?
When were the pivotal points beneficial?
When was there no positive change?
What were the reasons for that?
When did I as teacher cause pivotal points?
When did I do this out of an educational motive?
When did I do this out of an adult need?
How did I care for the child in both instances?
What came about in these situations?

27. Ether Body, Soul and 'I'

The ether body as educator

Experiences with the pivotal point show that we must handle our ether body more consciously when working with young children. The work demands that we don't just follow our own moods and urges, but also that we don't just do what the group wants, or a certain child wants. It is an art to use the ether body out of an insight in the situation. A Czech kindergarten teacher talked about different 'drawers' she could open or close. She meant that she had several inner attitudes she can call on to deal with different situations. You could also call them 'etheric friends' that appear as guides at different moments.

Sometimes a situation demands restraint, concentration, a more inward movement; sometimes it demands initiative, revitalising. Three particular skills are very important in this respect: learning to read situations; using the pedagogical chest of drawers; and the relationship between the two.

The soul and the ether body

When discussing pivotal points, it is very important to have a clear idea of the relationship between the ether body and the soul. We have to distinguish between this relationship in the upper part and the lower part of the human being.

In the upper pole, where the head is central, the ether body serves the consciousness-processes of the soul. For instance, if the soul wants to remember something, then the ether body as source of the memory helps it. But if we overindulge in impressions and images, the ether body will no longer be able to process and integrate them properly. Holes and half digested images appear that weaken the constitution and the consciousness. If we live with a question for a while and form thoughts about it, an insight may ripen, like a plant. We lovingly connect ourselves with a question and care for it with a lively attention. That requires a peaceful attitude and a certain restraint, qualities that are under pressure in our culture.

In the lower pole, the area of the stomach, metabolism and the limbs, we are asleep. Here the soul serves the etheric life processes that follow their own wisdom and order. If the soul uses the life forces in this area too much, in order to experience itself and to take pleasure in them, it will exhaust them: a life without rhythm, lots of sweets, unhealthy food, not enough rest and sleep, too much television, not enough movement. If such activities dominate, we lose our connection with the life forces and the feeling for what the body really needs, and our will-power is drained too. For young children who have not built up a stable life organism, this can be damaging.

So in all these areas it is important to have a feeling for the pivotal point, and to deal with it consciously.

Meditation

In the realm of consciousness we may experience a turning point toward a new connection if we do not follow our own familiar wish-images, but open ourselves up to the wisdom of the ether world. The soul has the capacity to concentrate and direct the attention. If it can manage to hold itself back with regard to the contents of thoughts and images, then the wise order of the ether world can reveal itself in our consciousness.

One example is logic. It demands inner discipline to follow a line of thought out of the coherence that is hidden in it. In the realm of mathematics, too (related to the chemical ether or ether of numbers) arbitrariness cannot be tolerated. The soul guides and concentrates the thinking attention, but lets itself be guided by the rules and logic inherent in mathematics. One and one is two, not three, although the latter might sometimes suit us better. The world of thoughts is an inwardly cohesive whole. In Ancient Greece it was called the *Logos*. The word Logos contains the concepts of both 'thought, thinking' and the 'word'. The Logos is the creative cohesion in the world that is spoken of at the beginning of the Gospel of St John: 'In the beginning was the word [the Logos].' The life ether is related to this. As we saw before, this is also called the word ether. If those relationships are respected, we can attain freedom by making meaningful connections and discovering our own insights. The endeavour to strive for insight and give it a direction is after all dependent on the individual.

So first we must restrain our own wishes and associations in our thinking. We can achieve this even stronger in meditation, where we open ourselves up to the spiritual world, which has its own inner cohesion and wisdom. The soul must first direct the attention with its will, for example to an image, a verse or an inner question. Then restraint is needed: an opening oneself up for what wants to come, not a filling of the inner space of this attention with a content. Georg Kühlewind called this attitude 'the gentle will'. It is the inverted will, the will become subservient, in the realm of consciousness.

This 'gentle will' is also needed to empathise with the being of a child. And here too, meditative exercises may help. We can, for example, summon up images of the children before going to sleep and take these images with us into the night. Or we can do this with a particular child about whom we have a question. In these ways we can open an inner space where the inner being of the child can speak out, for instance in the form of a dream, an idea, an endeavour, or perhaps in a gesture the child may make itself the following day. An answer can come in different ways, as we described in Chapter 6.

The 'I' has to educate the soul, as the soul educated the ether body. The 'I' can give a conscious direction to the soul, leading it in such a way that it restrains itself and opens up to the spiritual world.

Male and female ether body

It is probably no coincidence that there are hardly any male kindergarten teachers, in spite of emancipation and a striving for equality. I have not come across any in the Czech Republic or Slovakia. I met one in Holland and one in Germany, but they both went on to work with adults. What influence does the male and female constitution have on working in a 'caring' profession such as kindergarten teacher?

A very important indication Rudolf Steiner gave on the male and the female constitution is that the 'gender' of the ether body is the opposite of that of the physical body. So a male physical body has a female ether body and vice versa. What does this mean?

Although every human being is unique, we can observe general tendencies relating to gender. The male physical body expresses qualities such as being directed to the earth, to results, actively working from within towards the outer world. Male sexuality follows its own volition: new sperm cells are continuously produced.

Those are qualities we can recognise in the more active ether body of a woman. This ether body is more vital, more impulsive, more penetrating in the life of thinking.

The qualities associated with the female physical body are receiving, ripening and giving birth, enveloping, feeding, being held to regular rhythms. The egg cells are all present at birth, and are released in a regular rhythm. Those qualities are characteristic for the ether body of the man: in his thinking a man is more likely to strive for a cohesive image (like an egg-cell). He holds on to that, allowing him to 'hatch' a thought, a concept. Men are less flexible in reacting to a situation, and less likely to change their attitude. It was said of Lou Salome that each time she acquired a new lover, after nine months the lover bore a book.

It is very tempting to explore this fascinating theme further, but other authors (for instance, Gädeke) have done so before. We are interested in it here in what it means for our educational work, and in particular for the pivotal point. Women usually reach this pivotal point sooner in an environment without rhythms, focused on results. But then a pivotal point has a different, inverted value: it is not an opportunity to adapt, but more a moment to observe our own limitations and if possible to change the situation. That often requires a masculine, outwardly active attitude.

Many men reach a pivotal point at the mere thought of looking after small children. Nevertheless, more men are finding a connection to this sphere these days.

Both sexes have the task of developing complementary qualities and becoming whole as human beings (which is not the same as sacrificing the potential and values of one's own gender).

Everyone can ask themselves in which areas they reach their limits sooner than in others. In the process of developing the ether body as a pedagogical tool, each human being has a different constitutional starting point and their own potential and limitations. One polarity in this respect is the fundamental attitude of the masculine and the feminine. Perhaps this can be defined as being focused on the centre and focused toward the periphery. Focused on results or focused on caring. These are two fundamentally different attitudes. Obviously the peripheral attitude is extremely important for the education and care for young children, whether the carer is a man or a woman. Young children need a warm and safe environment.

Switching attitudes

Another problem posed by our culture is the need to switch. If we work in an office or factory all day, focused on efficiency, it is difficult to switch to a peripheral attitude, allowing things flow, find their own course, and to be present in a nourishing, supportive way. We will probably reach our limits quite quickly and may lack the flexibility to switch attitudes. How do we deal with that?

Working in an environment focused on results can give us a pleasant feeling: we are doing something tangible, achieving something, and are being paid and valued too. Letting go of that and being present in a different way can be difficult. Depending on work that is focused on results has dangers. We can get stuck in it and become workaholic. What if we fall ill? Then we are confronted with the one-sidedness of our attitude. But it may also be a chance to wake up to a deeper layer of our humanity, not dependent on outward results. There are lesser and greater pivotal points in life. Children, people with special needs, or the sick and elderly cannot compete in our culture. What happens to them? Are they worth less than others, are they any less human? Who has to experience a pivotal point in relation to them?

If we work at the same time as bringing up children, we have to create the conditions in which we can make that switch. For kindergarten teachers it is an issue too, how they can create the conditions for being present in their group in a covering, supportive way. Peace, regularity, rhythm and space, sufficient time to make transitions. Everyone can think of ways to manage this for themselves.

Metanoia

An illness or another outwardly restricting condition can lead to a pivotal point, and serve as a call to search out a different attitude to life. The outer circumstances themselves are not as important as our relationship to them. Set patterns of behaviour have usually become ingrained in the ether body. On the one hand that is necessary and a great help in many situations. On the other hand it can become a hindrance, for instance when the ingrained attitude does not fit the present situation, or if it is so one-sided that the organism suffers and falls ill. This tension between our ether body, and the demands of a situation, can cause our soul and 'I' to wake up. It may stimulate us to find a more suitable attitude to life or a more harmonious one. There are many examples, both in daily life and in great mythological images, which are also of great educational value.

St John's Tide in midsummer is one such image of a pivotal point. John the Baptist called on people to 'Change your ways'. The Greek *metanoia* is much broader than just 'Repent'. Over a period of time, this change in attitude or way can be made by the ether body, if the soul and the 'I' can come to an inner transformation and re-orientate themselves. St John asks us to re-orientate ourselves towards the spirit instead of to outer nature. It is no coincidence that St John's Tide is around the summer solstice. Outwardly nature is at the height of its appearance and begins to move toward autumn. If we hold on to our outward nature, we identify with what has 'crystallised' out in the ether and physical body, and we perish with it. But if we can find another starting point, a second human being may germinate that is not bound to mortal nature. This is not only the source for a new culture, but also for a renewal of the life forces in nature.

Questions for your own research

Three skills for handling pivotal points in a pedagogical way

1. Learning to read situations
After a pivotal point we have caused ourselves, we must ask: where was the group, where was the child?
Where did the process come from, where was it going to?
Why did I 'engineer' a pivotal point?

2. The pedagogical chest of drawers
Is my pedagogical chest of drawers (my circle of attitudes or 'etheric friends') well stocked?
What attitudes, which etheric friends do I have available as teacher?
Can I switch easily between these?
How can I fill and extend my chest of drawers?
Which drawers are well filled, which are missing?

3. *The relationship between both*
How did I make connections in the moment?
How did I transform my insight into what the situation demanded into the right attitude?
What effect did that have?
Looking back, could I have acted differently?

Meditation

Have I ever managed to take the image of a child with me into the night?
Did I relate that to a question?
What effect did that have?
Did I notice an effect on myself? In what form did that express itself?
Did I notice an effect on the child? In what form did that express itself?
Did I experience such 'answers' to my thoughts and feelings in other situations?
Am I open enough to notice such meaningful coincidences?
Do I do anything with them? How do I deal with them?
Do I let go of them, do I allow them to live on, do I try to enter into a direct conversation with them?
What experiences do I have with these various attitudes?

On male and female

When do I experience the particular qualities of my gender as a help?
When do I experience them as a hindrance or a challenge?
How does my gender influence my work with young children?
What expectations do I have of the opposite gender in education?
When am I present with my attention focused on the centre, when toward the periphery?
How do I judge that? How do I feel about that?
Can I switch between these two easily?
Do I have certain steps to help me make these transitions?

28. Afterword

We have reached the end of our journey through this book. The possibilities for exploration in the vast realm of the ether forces in education are not exhausted. This book offered some first impressions and initial explorations. It is a beginning, not a conclusion.

How the journey continues, readers may decide for themselves. No book can do the actual work for you. It is up to the will of the individual to what extent a new culture can come about in daily life. In courses and working with colleagues, all these things can be explored in a much livelier way than in a written text like this. Sharing impressions and doing movement exercises help to transform the concepts into experiences. Time and again we have seen that it also brings great joy and inspiration. Doing our own research can be exciting and help us move forward. Self discovered insights make us free and independent. We bring new life to our daily routine, which gives us energy to tackle the tasks and challenges of this wonderful work.

I hope the end of this book may for some readers be the beginning of their own journey. I'd love to hear about your impressions and experiences along the way. There are whole worlds waiting to be discovered.

Appendix: Some experiences from our workshops

Since 1998 we have worked with groups of kindergarten teachers and parents in further education and other courses, in the Czech Republic, Slovakia and in the Netherlands. Between seminars the participants research the questions daily in their classes.

Experiencing the etheric in movement

In these workshops I always do a series of exercises that allow participants to experience aspects of their own ether body. Some are movement exercises. Movement, the most direct medium, is very suitable for this. Simple exercises can help people gain insights and experience, which are of vital importance for working with a kindergarten group. To begin with, the exercises allow us to experience something of the etheric reality between the physical and the soul world. One of the most characteristic qualities of the etheric is for example the experience of the stream, of flow. The stream is in constant movement but still manages to hold itself together. If it becomes too fixed, too settled, it will tend to the physical. If it threatens to dissipate, become too nebulous, it tends toward the nature of the soul. In the stream itself we can, among other things, also experience the different qualitative relationships to time. How is our own ether body related to the stream of time? How does a communal time organism develop? By asking such questions and entering into such experiences, we discover qualities of our own ether body, such as the way we deal with the stream of time in a kindergarten group.

Our own ether body

We can find more objective qualities in the stream of time. If we open ourselves up to the stream of time in an unbiased way, four 'gates in time' will appear that lead to different 'experience-landscapes'. Everyone can perceive these during the exercises, even without any anthroposophical knowledge. The different affinities and sensitivities reveal something about the individual condition of the ether body of the participants. The four basic qualities are, however, universal and recognisable as the working of the four types of ether. We could characterise them as pulsating, orientating, rhythmicising and identifying (in movement as a medium for research). We can describe them differently, but they show the working of the warmth, light, chemical and life ethers.

Our own experiences can bring concepts to life, because the bridge between theory and practice of the ether world is our own ether body. Once we become attuned to them we can recognise the etheric qualities in ring games and folk songs, but also in free play and many other situations. We can then understand family or kindergarten activities in relation to their etheric qualities. With these insights we can create or adapt activities with pedagogical considerations in mind.

The schooling of teachers of young children

This brings us to a key problem in the training of teachers of young children. If we really want to develop the ether body in a purposeful way, we encounter the fact that we are actually asleep in our ether body. To consciously understand something of it, we must first bring something up out of the 'ether pond', so that we can see it and give it a name. But we do have to take it out of the pond. We often forget that we must then allow it to sink back into the ether pond to fructify our work with young children! If it remains in our consciousness as a concept, it will become estranged from its origins, like a fish dying on dry land. This paradox of working with the ether body is a central theme in the schooling of teachers of young children.

I came across one example of a kindergarten teacher who had done a certain exercise in one of our workshops. The session after that, she wanted to do that particular exercise again. She had experienced a situation in her group where she had been unable to cope. She had remembered the experience of the exercise and had been able to summon up its substance again. This helped her to bring the children back into the stream. When I asked her which exercise it was, she could not remember. Nor the reason why we had done it. But the experience had had such an effect on her, that she could recall the substance of it the moment she needed to, and use it.

This illustrates how the training of teachers of young children takes place on a totally different level from the training of teachers for older children. Training the latter, different parts of the human constitution come to the fore. The training of teachers of young children leads through the mostly unconscious realms of the world of young children. Generally our time and culture have lost all understanding of this. Consequently we hear about the education of young children as an increasing problem, because attempts are made to draw young children into the realm of adult consciousness as early as possible. But we cannot solve the problems with the same kind of thinking that caused them in the first place. To really understand young children, we must first unlock a human reality that lies deeper than the intellectual. Becoming more familiar with the ether world and nurturing it more consciously is the first task along that path.

The ideal of our courses is to create an 'inner workshop' where we learn to observe our own ether body and develop our own learning goals and strategies. In the workshops we share our methodical observations and experiences. Participants actually enjoy this communal searching and researching. They become more independent in their insights because they have gained and experienced these for themselves.

I strongly believe that in this day and age we can only progress if we actively search and research, using our own constitution as an instrument or tool of research, experiencing and developing it in the process.

Bibliography

Anschütz, Marieke, *Children and Their Temperaments*, Floris Books, UK 1995
Bockemühl, Jochen (ed.) *Toward a Phenomenology of the Etheric World*, SteinerBooks, USA 1985.
Bos, Lex, *Forming Judgments: A Path to Inner Freedom*, Ankerhus, 2006.
Burkhard, Gudrun, *Taking Charge: Your Life Patterns and Their Meaning*, Floris Books, UK 1997.
Gädeke, Wolfgang, *Sexuality, Partnership and Marriage*, Temple Lodge, UK 2009.
Houten, Coenraad van, *Awakening the Will: Principles and Processes in Adult Learning*, Temple Lodge Press, UK 2003.
Jaffke, Freya, *Celebrating Festivals with Children*, Floris Books, UK 2011
Jung, Carl Gustav, *Synchronicity*, London 1998.
Kühlewind, Georg, *The Gentle Will*, SteinerBooks, USA 2011.
Kutsch, Irgmard and Walden, Brigitte, *Spring Nature Activities for Children*, Floris Books, UK 2006
— *Summer Nature Activities for Children*, Floris Books, UK 2007
— *Autumn Nature Activities for Children*, Floris Books, UK 2005
— *Winter Nature Activities for Children*, Floris Books, UK 2006
Kornberger, Horst, *The Power of Stories: Nurturing Children's Imagination and Consciousness*, Floris Books, UK 2008
Leber, Stefan, *Die Menschenkunde der Waldorfpädagogik*, Freies Geistesleben, Stuttgart 1993.
Lindenau, Christof, *Der übende Mensch*, Freies Geistesleben, Stuttgart 1976.
Lievegoed, Bernard, *Phases of Childhood: Growing in Body, Soul and Spirit*, Floris Books, UK 1997.
Marti, Ernst, *The Four Ethers*, Schaumburg, USA 1984.
Marti, Ernst, *Das Ätherische*, Die Pforte, Dornach 1989.
Masters, Brien, *The Waldorf Song Book*, Floris Books, UK 1987.
Meyer, Rudolf, *The Wisdom of Fairy Tales*, Floris Books, UK 1995.
O'Neil, George and Gisela, *The Human Life*, Mercury Press, USA 1990.
Schoorel, Edmond, *The First Seven Years*, Rudolf Steiner College Press, USA 2004.

Sheldrake, Rupert, *Seven Experiments That Could Change the World*, Riverhead, London 1994.

Smyth, Nell, *The Breathing Circle: Learning Through the Movement of the Natural Breath*, Hawthorn Press, UK 2006.

Steiner, Rudolf, *The Education of the Child*, Anthroposophic Press, USA 1996.

Steiner, Rudolf, *Social Issues, Meditative Thinking and the Threefold Social Order* (CW 334), Anthroposophic Press, USA 1991.

Phases of Childhood

Growing in Body, Soul and Spirit

Bernard C J Lievegoed

Bernard Lievegoed takes a child's full humanity – body, soul and spirit – as his starting point. From this, a philosophy and pedagogy emerge in which, he argues, children can become happy, wise and skilled adults only when education takes the development of these three aspects into account from the very beginning.

Drawing on the educational ideas of Rudolf Steiner, and on a philosophical tradition going back to Goethe and Schiller, Lievegoed turns away from the materialist nineteenth-century notion of 'knowledge is power' which still pervades mainstream education today. He describes the three main stages of child development – pre-school, schoolchild and teenager – in a clear and concise way. Lievegoed shows that each stage of roughly seven years has its own character, and its own genetic and biographical potential.

The author goes on to explore the practical application of these insights as an education method in harmony with the child's developing relationship with the world around them.

www.florisbooks.co.uk

Celebrating Festivals with Children

Freya Jaffke

In this thoughtful book, Freya Jaffke describes festival celebrations in relation to child development in the first seven years. She considers in detail the main festivals throughout the year: Easter, Whitsun, St John's, starting school, harvest, Michaelmas, lantern time, birthdays, Halloween, Thanksgiving, Advent, Christmas, Epiphany and carnival.

Drawing on many examples, she shows how we can celebrate festivals with children at home and in kindergarten in a meaningful way. Every festival is prefaced with a deeper contemplation for adults, before considering preparations with children, followed by the actual organisation of the festival – with games, craft activities and decorations, stories, songs, poems and the seasonal nature table.

www.florisbooks.co.uk

Children and their Temperaments

Marieke Anschütz

Drawing on an ancient tradition, Rudolf Steiner referred to four fundamental 'types' or 'temperaments' in the human personality, each of which, he said, has different personal needs and ways of relating socially.

From her experience of working with children of all ages, Marieke Anschütz provides a guide to children's different temperaments and their role in child character, health and personality development.

The book includes illustrations from home and school, in the context of the Steiner-Waldorf classroom. The author discusses how these ideas may be used to manage, and relate to, groups and individuals.

www.florisbooks.co.uk

Irmgard Kutsch & Brigitte Walden
ISBN 978–086315–544–4

Irmgard Kutsch & Brigitte Walden
ISBN 978–086315–586–4

Irmgard Kutsch & Brigitte Walden
ISBN 978–086315–495–9

Irmgard Kutsch & Brigitte Walden
ISBN 978–086315–564–2

Ideal for Steiner-Waldorf Kindergartens and Schools

www.florisbooks.co.uk